CHRISTMAS STYLE

DEBI STARON AND BOB PRANGA

PHOTOGRAPHY BY DAVID MAGER

DK PUBLISHING, INC.

DK

LONDON, NEW YORK, MELBOURNE
MUNICH, DELHI

Senior Editor Barbara Berger
Assistant Managing Art Editor Michelle Baxter
Editorial Assistant John Searcy
Additional Design Tai Blanche, Melissa Chung,
Susan St. Louis, Stephanie Sumulong, and Miesha Tate
DTP Coordinator Milos Orlovic
Production Manager Chris Avgherinos
Jacket Design Dirk Kaufman
Project Director Sharon Lucas
Creative Director Tina Vaughan
Publisher Chuck Lang

Photography David Mager
Photographic Assistants Monica Morant,
Beth Coller, Charchi Stinson

First American Edition 2004
04 05 06 07 10 9 8 7 6 5 4 3 2 1

Published in the United States by
DK Publishing, Inc.
375 Hudson Street
New York, New York 10014

DK Publishing offers special discounts for bulk purchases for sales
promotions of premiums. Specific, large-quanity needs can be
met with special editions, including personalized covers,
excerpts of existing guides, and corporate imprints.
For more information, contact:
Special Markets Department
DK Publishing, Inc.
375 Hudson Street
New York, New York 10014
Fax: 212-689-5254

Cataloging-in-Publication data is available
from the Library of Congress
ISBN: 0-7566-0556-3

Color reproduction by Colourscan, Singapore
Printed and bound by Toppan Printing Co. (Shenzhen) Ltd.

See our complete product line at
www.dk.com

CONTENTS

FOREWORD

IT'S LIKE A BIG CRESCENDO of emotions, that's what the holiday season is. We spend so much time building the notes higher, and higher, and higher, and when we reach the top we want to try to hold those notes for as long as we possibly can. The memory of it is so powerful and so delicious that we try to recreate it year after year. Most of us try to capture at least part of the experience from our childhoods. I guess that's why I have come to rely on Bob and Debi—Dr. Christmas—to help orchestrate the holiday for me.

It's a delicate balance; a little bit of tradition, add some whimsy, heavy on meaning and substance; then bring in legacies and color. Finally, when all of those notes are ringing in complete harmony, make it work on time and on a budget! It's no wonder that, as the conductor of that orchestra, we're often frustrated and feel like failures.

I first met Bob when I was hosting and producing my talk show—he was a slam-dunk guest. Every time he came on, it was a self-produced masterpiece that really resonated with my viewers because he always found a way to make the holiday accessible and affordable. We all know, of course, in our heart of hearts, that the trimming and the glistening of ornaments, and the stockings, the centerpieces, the wreaths, and all the rest are merely window dressing for what is to most people a deeply religious season. But without it, it sure seems empty and lackluster—and that is *not* Bob Pranga.

I must confess to being a little nervous the first time Bob came over to my home with his little team of elves to transform my living room and dining room. But now, after many years of depending upon his skill and taste, I can't image the holiday without him. Bob and Debi manage to consider whatever Christmas means to each client—celebrity or otherwise. No matter how big the star, there is always a young child behind all those accomplishments wanting to recapture that excitement of the holiday.

Bob took ornaments that my kids had made in grade school—popsicle sticks and yarn held together by Elmer's glue and topped with a handful of glitter—and somehow managed to make them coexist beautifully with handmade, mouth-blown, one-of-a-kind ornaments. If I tell him a picture is important, he finds a way to showcase it. If I want some of the kids' toys and keepsakes to mix in with the fine china and candles, voilà, there they are.

I will never forget returning from Palm Springs one weekend after Bob and Debi had done their magic—

▲ **Heavenly table** A detail of the "dense forest of birch trees . . . set among the clouds, ready for a peace banquet," created by Dr. Christmas for Leeza Gibbons.

I opened the door, and chill bumps— there it was—that feeling from my girlhood.

I think the thing that is most amazing about a Dr. Christmas holiday is the care that goes into every decision. While they make it appear effortless, Debi and Bob obsess over every detail. They love to share their passion with others, easily chatting about everything from the right lighting, to proper placement of the tree, to the color scheme.

One year, I was providing a report to air on *Extra* about celebrity trees. Debi was passing on the art of weaving ribbon throughout the branches of the tree. Of course, I needed the sound bite in about 30 seconds, so she went into "warp speed" to explain the kind of ribbon to use, how to place it on the tree, and how to economize if you needed to! Bob is always the emotional glue, providing punctuation for Debi's practical tips.

On these pages you'll see how versatile and talented these two really are. You'll understand why many stars depend on them and why most don't even question the process. They just say "do it" and trust that it will be the perfect representation of individuality and taste.

This year, I just decided to "trust the process" and turned over my home to the Dr. Christmas team for a couple of days. Who knew my dining room would vanish? It was replaced by a dense forest of birch trees and a heavenly table set among the clouds, ready for a peace banquet. Twinkling lights and illuminated snowbanks made the whole scene look like something out of an adult's holiday dream. I cried when I saw it and then made all my friends come over and experience a bit of the magic. That's when you know you got it right—when someone can stand at the entry and behold this magnificent vision so powerful it can only provoke a deeply felt "Ahhh." There are no words. Well, maybe two: Dr. Christmas.

Leeza Gibbons

LEEZA GIBBONS

AUTHORS' PREFACE

Hello, everyone. We are Dr. Christmas—Debi Staron and Bob Pranga. We're not a medical corporation. We *are* specialists of Christmas and have decorating ideas and tips to share, and the holidays are fast approaching. But before getting started, we'd like to take this opportunity to tell you about our approach to decorating, and to introduce you to some of the people who have contributed to this book, and influenced and enhanced our lives.

...from Debi

Debi and her dad, Ted

*M*y earliest memories of Christmas are of sitting in Santa's lap in the local shopping mall and of helping my dad, the "Master" of outdoor Christmas decorating, as he strung lights from antenna tip to basement window. My dad did the best Christmas decorations. People drove for miles around to see his display. I still remember the look on his face as he watched the faces of the neighbors, who marveled at his creative expertise. Having developed a similar passion for decorating, I consider it an honor to carry on the fine tradition of Christmas decorating, on a "slightly" grander scale. To him, my inspiration, my teacher, and my Christmas guide, I dedicate this book.

I would also like to thank Dr. Howard Maize, D.C., client and healer, for helping to keep me "upright" so I'm able to do what I do, and for his kind words: "Finally, a book that depicts, even if just a sampling, the magic that is Dr. Christmas. After having the unique experience of actually watching Deborah set up my office for the past several Christmases, I have been in awe of her innate ability to set just the right, the exact mood for our needs. Her flair, her expertise, elan, panache . . . are a sight to behold!"

...from Bob,

*W*hen one is presented with a great opportunity, it's easy to settle into the mindset of "It's about time". . . I have to admit to being guilty as charged. When asked about my dedication for this book, I had to get real about how I got here. It's amazing how much the "I" is not a part of the equation. I dedicate this book as follows:

To my family, especially my parents, who passed their love of Christmas on to me. To my mentors and other "moms," Judy Andruss, Connie

Bob and his friend Ben McCormick

Pentek, and Patricia Strang, for your faith, tenacity, and life experiences. To Kathy Hilton, whose belief in my abilities opened the doors. To Julia Finlay and Judy Merrell, your influences I still carry with me. To my coach, Rick Tamlyn, for changing my life. To Chuck Lioi, for giving the world the big "scoop" about us. To Susan Ranta, my friend and muse. To Molly Lewis, who keeps me laughing. To Dayna Jackson, for keeping me clear. To my Los Angeles family, thank you for being part of the journey. And to Ben McCormick, my friend and fellow dreamer. One dream down, more to follow.

IF YOU'RE TRYING to figure out what a "Dr. Christmas" tree looks like, stop. We don't have one single style, theme, or way of decorating. What we are presenting is a combination Traditional Christmas-look / Trendy-style showcase / Over-the-top fun gallery.

We describe how we achieved each look so that you can recreate it in your own home. And we explain in more detail how to tackle certain projects, with accompanying step-by-step, easy-to-follow photos.

If you've always wanted to turn your tree into something more than a green, bushy holder for your ornament collection, we'll show you how. Over the years, we've learned that with tree decorating, anything goes—we've wired the most amazing assortment of things into trees: diamond tiaras, sports equipment, mannequins, framed celebrity pictures, toys, curtain rods, train sets, furniture, and even a wedding dress!

You can put just about anything you want into your tree, as long as the tree can support the weight. Don't limit yourself to traditional themes—break loose and experiment.

Okay, we have said "Hello" and explained the Dr. Christmas philosophy; now for the introductions. First, meet Donald Clay. We brought Donald on board because of his expertise in floral design. He was excited to conjure up the decorated trees based on the ideas we had for the floral chapter. Donald's use of flowers and fruit was incredibly innovative and exceeded our expectations. For that we thank him.

Donald Clay

Now meet chef Richard Rocha. All of the scrumptious desserts and pastries featured throughout the book may be credited to him. We provided him with the themes and moods we wished to achieve and he delivered the appropriate fare. Kudos.

Chef Richard Rocha

Finally, our able and overworked helpers, the Elves: Garry Kubel, Jay Krich, Lynn Klein, Gail Jorden, Brent Braun, and Brent Bateman (who is missing from the photograph below).

The Elves, from the left: Garry Kubel, Jay Krich, Lynn Klein, Gail Jorden, Brent Braun

They are the backbone of Dr. Christmas. Without them, we're nothing. The same is true for all of the fantastic people who we call our clients. These are the folks who have allowed us time and time again to "play" in their beautiful homes and show them off to the world. Bette and Scott Milne, Barron and Marilyn Hilton, Carrie Fisher, Candice Bergen, Teri Garr, Marion and David Dennis, Ilene Graham, Richard Bronson, Edie Baskin-Bronson, Larry and Dee Dee Gordon, Martin and Wen Mull, Jillian Barberie, Kevin Bailey and James Mellon, Tracy Thompson, Karen, and our angel, Leeza Gibbons.

Debi Staron

Bob Pranga

1

THE ART OF HOLIDAY DESIGN

*O*nce, decorating for Christmas meant picking out a tree, stringing several lights, and hanging a few balls and garlands. But no more. Christmas has now become a spectacular art form. The broad array of quality decorations in many assorted colors now rival those exhibited in couture fashion. In fact, in recent years, Christmas trends have begun to follow fashion trends. Christmas is no longer limited to just red and green, but is now all about artistic expression. Enjoy!

Traditional

STYLES OF DECORATING that have been around for many years, and trimmings in colors and shapes of seemingly timeless appeal—these are elements of what is known as "Traditional" Christmas design. Examples of popular traditional tone-setters include both the classic color combinations of primary red and green with round or bell-shaped ornaments; and Victorian burgundy, forest green, and mauve with feminine ornaments, angels, and Father Christmas motifs. The following pages feature examples of traditional design created for today's home.

TRADITIONAL LUXURY

TAILORED, COLOR-COORDINATED, AND CRISP describe Upscale Traditional design. Red is a color featured in most traditional Christmas displays— make your design upscale by mixing red with silver and gold instead of other primary colors, and replace cotton and paper with higher-quality materials like silk, brocade, and velvet.

Here, we used custom-made velvet ribbon to create large, full bows that were placed on everything from mirror garlands to alcoves to stairways and trees—carrying the luxurious theme throughout. The ornament selection included mouth-blown one-of-a-kind pieces rather than mass-produced decorations.

When decorating in Upscale-Traditional style, think clean lines and sophisticated luxury. The end result: an impressive, decor-enhancing Christmas showcase.

▲ **Decorative alcove** This nook, which is adjacent to the entrance, was outlined with a garland and decorated to match the hallway in order to continue the clean line of the overall design.

▶ **Meet and greet** These two large brass deer serve as holiday greeters at the front entrance. To dress these everyday reindeer for the season, red ribbon collars and jingle bells were fitted around their necks.

◀ **Framing potential** The traditional color palette of red and green enhances an already-grand entry hall. The red ribbon, greenery, and twinkling lights lead you on a journey down the long hall to the main attraction, the elegant family tree in the drawing room, where the window makes a natural frame.

MAJESTIC STATEMENT

This magnificent tree rises twelve feet from floor to ceiling. It serves several functions during the holiday season for the family who lives in this mansion: it acts as the center of attention for family parties, it is the glamorous backdrop for the annual family Christmas card, and, of course, it is the exciting place where everyone gathers on Christmas morning to open their fabulous presents.

Every year, the tree goes up on December 1 and is taken down after New Year's Day—because a live tree would lose its luster long before Christmas, and since the tree sits in direct sunlight, a prelit artificial tree is used. Clear lights create an upscale look. Red-velvet ribbon continues the statement begun in the entrance hallway, and a red-velvet tree skirt provides an inviting stage on which gifts will be displayed.

▶ **Hearts on display** This 3-D heart, made from metal wire and red-glass beads, allows the twinkling light to shine through. Its shiny silver frame reflects the lights and provides additional sparkle.

▲ **Porcelain poinsettias** Enhancing the silver bells and white, beaded-silk ribbon, this porcelain ornament combines all the colors used on the tree. It also adds a sophisticated touch to a recognizable Christmas staple, the Christmas poinsettia.

▶ **Treasures of Egypt** Handcrafted Egyptian glass adds upscale Middle-Eastern flair to the tree. The 18-carat gold that has been applied to the etched glass counterbalances the silver metallic wire of the red-beaded heart. Its unusual shape is eye-catching.

◀ **Silver bells** This lovely collectible silver wedding bell sits amid a swirl of beaded-silk ribbon. Several bells were placed throughout the tree. These bells and the white ribbon are complementary elements that set off the large red bows, the principal statement pieces.

▶ **Center of attention** Framed in this dramatic window setting, all eyes are immediately drawn to this fabulous spectacle of Egyptian glass, 18-carat-gold-and-crystal ornaments, designer porcelains, and crystal-bead garlands. Gold icicles add vertical lines, encouraging the eye to travel up and down the height of the tree.

STUNNING SPIRAL

When you arrive at this house, upon entering the grand hallway, two choices present themselves: a right turn will take you to the drawing room with its twelve-foot-tall tree. A left turn, however, will bring you here, to this spiral staircase and beautiful crystal chandelier.

Therefore, we decided to place a smaller version of the drawing-room tree next to this stairway. The red-velvet ribbon continues the "through-line" (a decorating term referring to a fabric, color, or ornament that is repeated in a design to tie the look together) to this end of the house. Since the stairway, the grand hallway, and the drawing room can all be seen at the same time, it was important to create uniformity. By doing so, one long, continuous flow of red, silver, and gold was achieved.

The hand-carved wooden stairway designed by renowned Los Angeles architect Paul Revere Williams demanded special attention, so it was draped with several pieces of lush garland, matching that used in the hall. Red bows, twinkling lights, and crystal ornaments help lead the eye up the stairs.

▶ **Golden orb** The only one of its kind on the tree, this piece was chosen for its simple elegance. The gold is in keeping with the theme colors chosen, but the unique shape stands out.

▲ **Velvet elegance** A tree was needed at this end of the house in order to balance the total design, because decorated alone, the stairway was not a strong enough statement. Everything on this tree was made on a smaller scale than on the main tree—from the bows and garlands to the tree skirt.

▼ **Beaded star** This beaded treetop star is a companion piece to the beaded ornaments. Normally found at the top of the tree, here it shares the spotlight with the true stars of the tree, the dramatic red ribbons and bows.

▶ **Ornate beading** In place of the white beaded ribbon used on the main family tree, these custom-crafted silk-and-glass-bead ornaments were hung on the staircase tree. This gave the tree a feeling similar to that of its larger counterpart, but a unique style.

◀ **View from above** Looking down from the second-floor landing, the eye is treated to a different perspective. When you peek down through the crystal chandelier to the polished marble floor, the tree is seen as the major focal point, which is intimately wrapped up in this famous stairway.

VICTORIAN INFLUENCE

VICTORIAN DESIGN IS UNIQUE—it is the only Christmas look named after a historical era. Although Christmas trees were introduced to Britain by Victoria's grandmother, Queen Charlotte, it was Queen Victoria's consort, Albert—a German prince—who popularized the custom of decorating trees. Victoria and Albert decorated their trees with glass ornaments imported from Germany, alongside candies, wax dolls, fruit and nuts, and candles for illumination. Other elements used in Victorian Christmas-tree design included small toys, paper ornaments, and ribbon, and the colors were dark jewel tones. When this look came to America, it was softened by the addition of pinks and mauves, giving Victorian Christmas a more feminine feel.

◀ **Pastels in paper** The pink hydrangeas on the tree were introduced in order to create floral highlights. The "vases" —paper Victorian-motif cones—could also be used to hold candies and other sweets.

◀ **A royal dining experience** Traditional Victorian Christmas tables served up boar, roast beef, and mince-meat pie. Set here at a flower-laden modern table with Victorian influence, bone china and lace placemats stand ready to present a more contemporary meal. A small floral-themed tree nestles in a garlanded bay window; live plants grace the chandelier, and a dried wreath hangs on a side door.

▲ **Victorian rose** Designer-silk chair wraps were used to disguise the homeowners' chairs, which were not suited to the Victorian style. The rosette tied on the back is in keeping with the room's floral theme.

◀ **Village charm** This Victorian church and tavern are parts of an illuminated snow village that adds charm to the sideboard. Victorians often created tableaux on their Christmas tables; now they can be an upscale way of displaying your collectible villages.

REGAL HOLIDAY BANQUET

Color was the motivation for selecting the decorative pieces displayed in the dining room. Instead of using the traditional Victorian dark jewel tones, lighter colors such as pink, cream, fuchsia, and mint green were used to soften the dark, heavy wood. Silks, brocades, velvets, porcelains, ceramics, and glass were blended with paper, tin, and live flowers to create a delicate and romantic feeling.

This room was dressed for an elaborate holiday party, so every surface in the room was decorated, including pedestals and door arches—even the food platters were embellished. A gourmet pastry chef was commissioned to make beautiful, elegant desserts that were appropriate for the theme.

The windows, buffets, and pedestals were all festooned in artificial greenery lit with clear, twinkling lights. Burgundy and emerald-green velvet bows provide a regal accent.

▶ **Sugared teacakes** A silver serving dish garnished with leaves and crystal twigs gives these cakes special distinction. They were designed to look like miniature presents, right down to the narrow ribbons and tiny bows.

▲ **Christmas-tree confection** "Sugarcoated" with glitter so that it looks good enough to eat, this stunning glass piece is whimsically colorful, with pastel green, red, pink, and purple flowers, bows, and sashes.

▶ **Hearts and flowers** Romance is embodied in this delicate glass heart, hand-painted with leaves and flowers. During the romantic Victorian era, hearts were a popular motif.

▶ **Victoriana on stage** (far right) The main buffet needed a strong dramatic statement. A miniature stage with bright-red curtains and gold trim was a perfect set for an angelic Victorian vision.

▶ **Old-world charm** (top left) This Father Christmas earthenware figurine is a cleverly sculpted teapot.
▶ **Merry minstrel** (top right) Green velvet bows top a decorative pedestal wrapped in a thick garland with twinkling clear lights.
▶ **Rich brocade** (bottom left) A feminine fabric ornament helps soften the darkness of the tree.
▶ **Porcelain in pink** (bottom right) Two finely crafted porcelain drops hang side by side. The delicate floral motif echoes the romantic theme.

VICTORIAN INNOCENCE

Toys were common decorations on Victorian Christmas trees. Our model for this tree was a giant dollhouse, so the vision for this design was simple: Start with one special collectible, feature her prominently at the top of the tree, and surround her with doll friends and a collection of red hats so they can play dress-up. Since all of the dolls were dressed in their winter finery, we chose a frosted artificial tree that looked as if it was dusted with snow.

White faux fur is a common element on the dolls' costumes, the fabric ornaments, and the oversized matching tree skirt. (When outfitting a large tree, it is important to use a skirt big enough to extend beyond the bottommost branches of the tree to balance the design.)

In order to share this Victorian vision with neighbors, we opened the curtains and tied them back with maroon crushed-velvet ribbon. Intricately carved Bavarian wood pieces depicting Christmas scenes brighten the dark windows.

▶ **Father Christmas** A rosy-cheeked glass Saint Nicholas ornament carries a tiny tree and gold-wrapped present.

◀ **Toyland** Bay windows are excellent tree locations, allowing you to to create a tableau, away from the flow of traffic. Because dolls are the principal focal points on this tree, miniature pieces of doll furniture—satin lamps and velvet chairs—were added to support the theme. Pink and maroon bead garlands tie in to the Victorian colors used in the dining room (previous pages).

▶ **White fur** The faux-fur trimming on this ornament mimics the fluffy collars on the dolls' dresses, while the winter-red fabric stands out against the frosty branches. An airy top bow contrasts with the heavier brocade.

▲ **Versatile greenery** One wreath hangs traditionally in the center of the window, while another lies atop a grand piano to create a stunning centerpiece. Victorian lampposts, tea lights, and a large pillar candle in a beaded candleholder illuminate the area with a romantic glow.

◀ **Fringed footwear** A collection of miniature Victorian-style floral shoe ornaments continues the "dolly dress-up" motif.

▲ **Victorian bonnet** Doll-size hats—little girls' playthings—adorn the tree. Like Victorian hats, they are decorated with a mix of ribbon, lace, flowers, or feathers.

ANGELIC TABLEAU

A decorated stairway can become a background that adds interest to your tree display. Matching the staircase trimming to the tree gives your design area a coordinated look. As this is the entry hall, a rich Victorian tableau was created to set the theme for the entire home.

Hunter green and burgundy are traditional Victorian tones. Angels, velvet ribbons, paper ornaments, and miniature flowerpots complete the theme. The bright-red angel gives this rather dark corner a dramatic lift. If this tree were truly from Victorian times, candles would have been used as illumination. Although they cast a romantic glow, candles are a fire hazard and are not recommended.

▲ **Framed portrait** It was common practice to use colorful pictures and postcards as decorative flourishes in Victorian times. This antique postcard has a period feel.

▶ **Celestial movement**
These angels were designed with movable joints, allowing you to change their positions and place them in a variety of poses.

▶ **Heavenly angels**
Angels have traditionally been used only as treetoppers. However, flying several of them throughout the tree—and even in the garland—lends an illusion of movement, while Santa in his sleigh keeps the tree grounded.

▲ **First look** The front door is the first thing your guests will see. By placing a decorative wreath out front, you give them a prelude to the grand overture waiting inside. This wreath features a maroon crushed-velvet bow made of ribbon, which is used throughout the interior design.

▲ **Lamplight** For a party—on a clear night—try tying a simple bow on existing exterior light fixtures. Here, alongside a stone garden cherub, nothing more was needed but a sprinkling of clear lights in the background, which created a lovely starlight effect.

Celebrations

THE WINTER MONTHS are a popular time of the year for grand celebrations in many different cultures around the world: some are religious festivals, some celebrate bounteous gifts, and some are remembrances of ancient miracles. All of them share common bonds—they are times of loving, sharing, and giving thanks with family and friends. Here we celebrate these special moments.

COMBINED TRADITIONS

IMAGINE THAT SOMEWHERE DEEP in a winter forest sits a magical table covered in snow, illuminated by candles, and dressed for a feast, in anticipation of the day when the world's great cultures unite in peace. Here, we created a whimsical and elegant "winter wonderland" dining room with crystal accents, where Christmas, Hanukkah, and Kwanzaa—and other winter holidays such as Id-ul-Fitr, celebrated at the end of the Islamic month of Ramadan, or Bodhi Day, the anniversary of Buddha's enlightenment—can be celebrated together.

One way to decorate your home for an interfaith or intercultural holiday celebration that respects different religions, communities, and customs is to use a neutral color like white as a unifying theme. White can also serve as a backdrop for the introduction of other colors associated with these various holiday traditions, such as blue for Hanukkah; or red, black, and green for Kwanzaa.

◀ **Celebrating together** Family members and friends of all faiths can break bread together in this fantasy setting. The illusion of a forest was created with birch trees trimmed in crystal-and-white ornaments and clear lights, surrounding a table and chairs covered in faux-fur fabric and flocked with cotton "snow" batting.

▼ **Mixing symbols** In keeping with the theme of unity, neutral crystal was chosen for the centerpiece elements: a dreidel for Hanukkah, a Kwanzaa cup, and a Christian nativity scene, all arranged together on a layer of artificial snow.

ELEGANT ICE

No one does it better than Mother Nature when it comes to winter design. Pure white snow and the sparkle of ice crystals put even the most spectacular diamond to shame. It's a hard act to follow, but it can be done using the right blend of acrylics, porcelain, and crystal glass. Remember, nature isn't perfect, so try to use ornaments, garlands, and decorative pieces that have unique textures, shapes, and sizes. Incorporating elements of nature such as live tree branches, pine cones, and winter berries will enhance your display. Try using several mirrors in your design: mirrored ornaments and wall mirrors that hang or lean near your display not only reflect the sparkle of lights and crystal, they can also add depth and dimension. Lastly, a thick blanket of snow provides the finishing touch to any winter wonderland. Here, we used pieces of rolled-cotton batting, rounded their edges, and added a fine dusting of artificial snow.

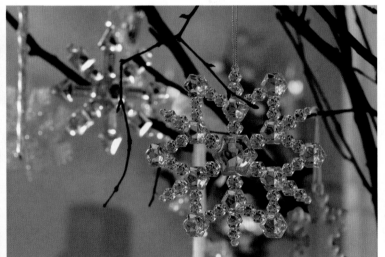

▲ **Winter star** This majestic acrylic star makes a dramatic statement with its size and shape. Its straight, crisp, distinct lines and pointed rays stand out against the naturally irregular branches. When using large heavy decorations on thin branches, make sure the trees can support the weight, and never place them directly over the heads of your guests.

▶ **Frosty fashion** We added high-end elegance to the display with the help of this fabric-covered ornament. The highly detailed piece combines silk and satin ribbons, beaded tassels, silver braiding, and a sophisticated pattern.

▲ **A hint of blue** This acrylic snowflake introduces a subtle daub of color to the white canvas and increases the wintry feeling. Its color also represents Hanukkah; honor different holidays by adding decorations in traditional colors.

◀ **Graceful porcelain** Delicate designs cover this collectible porcelain ornament. Its unusual urn shape conveys an element of grace to the overall design, so several pieces were hung thoughout the display.

▶ **Snowy glen** A forest of crystal and snow rests atop this elegant buffet. Three white candles sit nestled in a wreath of ice crystals. Pearl garlands strung randomly from tree branches create an elegant necklace for this winter wonderland.

CHRISTMAS

It all started with a baby in a manger. Everything that is Christmas began with one special moment in time—the birth of Christ in Bethlehem more than two thousand years ago. The grandeur of Christmas is showcased in this dramatic living room, which we decorated with Christian religious symbols and icons associated with the Holy Family and the Nativity.

The tree was decorated to match the room's color scheme, which supported traditional spiritual tones: royal purple, midnight blue, matte gold, and creamy white. To give the design a warm, earthy feel, we selected a live tree. This tree was too full to allow us to adequately display many of the large pieces we chose to showcase, so we added live manzanita branches in several locations to provide needed display space and to break up the natural line of the tree. To complete the look, we framed the windows behind the tree with lit garlands that were left undecorated, so they would not pull focus from the tree itself.

◀ **Glorious angel** In the tree, angels of different ethnicities symbolize universal acceptance. The theme was tied together with gold satin, emulating the angels' robes.

▶ **Ship of the desert** Carrying the nativity theme from tabletop to tree, this molded-glass camel presents an interesting shape.

▼ **Away in a manger** The Nativity scene is the most well-known Christmas religious symbol. This large Nativity set was placed on a table near the tree.

▲ **Cross** Although the empty cross is actually an Easter symbol, symbolizing Jesus's resurrection, the jewel colors on this ornament perfectly accent the tree.

◀ **The Magi** The Gospels tell of three wise men who rode camels from eastern lands, following a star to Bethlehem to see the baby Jesus. The scene is hand-painted on this gold glass ornament, fitting the Nativity theme well in both color and subject matter.

▼ **Heralding angel** This molded-glass, handpainted piece was suspended from a branch to give the appearance of flight.

HANUKKAH

In Hebrew, "Hanukkah" means dedication, and its celebration commemorates the rededication of the Temple in Jerusalem more than two thousand years ago, after it was destroyed by foreign invaders. The legend of Hanukkah, known as the Festival of Lights, tells of how a small army of Jews led by Judah Maccabee won back the temple, only to find one day's supply of oil left to light the gold menorah (a Jewish religious candelabra); miraculously it burned for eight days. Today, candles are used instead of oil.

Blue is the primary color associated with Hanukkah (it is considered a holy, royal color in Judaism), and it is typically mixed with silver, gold, or white. Here, we combined the symbols of Hanukkah—the menorah, the dreidel (a spinning top), and the Star of David—into a striking display for a Hanukkah party. A shiny silver tree with crystal-drop accents was added to give height to the display and provide a unique "Festival of Lights."

▲ **Star of David** A delicate glass Star of David hangs proudly. The six-pointed star, an ancient symbol believed to have magical properties, was not officially adopted as a symbol of Judaism until the 1700s.

◄ **Menorah** An elegant silver menorah is a stunning decoration for this holiday table. On each of the eight nights of Hanukkah, an extra candle is lit. The center candle is used to light the others.

◄ **Temple** This electrically lit porcelain building is a modern part of the decorating scheme. It is a model of New York Central Synagogue (c. 1839), the oldest Jewish house of worship in continuous use in New York City and a magnificent example of American synagogue architecture.

▲ **Dreidel and gelt** This crystal dreidel adds sparkle to the table amid a sea of chocolate gelt ("money" used in the dreidel game). The dreidel is engraved with Hebrew letters meaning "A miracle happened here." The game dates back to the Maccabees.

▶ **Festive table** Twinkling candlelight casts a glow on this decorative table created for an intimate Hanukkah gathering. To honor the holiday's roots, the large candle featured on the table is actually an oil candle, filled with decorative foliage in tones of silver and blue.

KWANZAA

The African-American and Pan-African holiday of Kwanzaa, which celebrates the reaffirmation of family, community, and culture, was founded in 1966. The name "Kwanzaa" is from the Swahili phrase *matunda ya kwanza,* meaning "first fruits," and Kwanzaa's origins are rooted in celebrations of the harvest that have been practiced by African peoples since the time of Ancient Egypt and Nubia.

When designing this room for a Kwanzaa gathering, we wanted to emphasize the warm feeling of celebrating one's community. It seemed appropriate to beautify this home's living-room fireplace, the heart of the house. The rustic, brick fireplace signifies warmth and lends itself to displaying traditional Kwanzaa elements, such as a cornucopia, a candle-holder, and a Unity Cup. The colors of Kwanzaa—red, black, and green—flow beautifully against the red stone background.

▶ **Unity Cup** This wooden goblet, called the *Kikombe cha Umoja,* symbolizes the principle of unity. It is placed front and center on a mat called a *Mkeka,* which represents the foundation of African cultural history.

◀ **Harvest hearth** Putting a new spin on fireplace decorations, colorful African fabrics and red and green ribbons were incorporated into the design.

▼ **First fruit** These fruits and vegetables represent the bounty of the harvest. Glass vegetable ornaments were interspersed with the real ones, to add glitter to the display.

▲ **Ornamental accent** Picking up two of the traditional colors of Kwanzaa, this holiday ball nestles in the artificial pine garland and an African-textile-patterned ribbon.

◀ **Candles** The Kwanzaa candleholder is known as a *Kinara.* A symbol of ancestral Africa, it holds seven candles that stand for the seven principles of Kwanzaa: unity, self-determination, collective work and responsibility, cooperative economics, purpose, creativity, and faith. Red represents the struggle for freedom, black represents the people, and green represents both the harvest and hope for the future.

All That Glitters

ALL THAT GLITTERS is gold—and much more. Metallic hues—from silver, platinum, copper, and brass to every jewel-tone imaginable—sparkle and shimmer, mirroring the bright lights of the holiday season. The upscale quality of polished metal provides a spectacular, sumptuous display, rich in color and dramatic in design. Lights and candles play an important role in glittery decor, providing extra points of light that dance beautifully off the many reflective surfaces.

GOLDEN OPULENCE

GOLD, ACCENTED WITH OTHER METALLIC COLORS—platinum, silver, and copper—brings this design to life. A one-color scheme would have flattened the overall look of the white tree, but the combination of two or more colored metals gives the tree depth and "pop" against its mostly white surroundings.

Drama is the key element for a metallic look. Choose shiny, bright, and glittered or sequined pieces—anything that will reflect light. The beauty of designing with gold is its versatility. Adding an accent color creates a different mood, and you can vary colors from year to year. The addition of black, as seen in the tree on the next page, can be quite dramatic and adds richness.

◀ **Silver and gold trimmings** Handmade fabric ornaments and handpainted glass pieces hang on the blank canvas of a white tree, while countless twinkling lights are reflected in the polished marble floor of this classical room setting. Matching sleigh, tree skirt, and garlanded pillars add to the sparkle.

◀ **Matte softness** The matte finish and polished veneer of this white-and-gold ornament works well to balance the more striking metallic elements on the tree. Topped with a gold ribbon, it gives the tree a soft shine and adds depth.

▲ **Striking the right chord** A faux-jewel-accented gold harp is in perfect harmony with the angelic surroundings. Relating decorations to one another, such as placing this harp next to a neighboring angel, lets you tell a story within your decorating scheme.

◀ **Perfect placement** This angel stands in the center of a wreath on an entry-way table, instead of on the treetop. An angel, a figurine—or even a pretty bowl of ornaments—can be set in a table wreath to create a festive centerpiece.

DECADENT DESIGN

Individually, black, gold, silver, and pearls are colors and jewels associated with wealth and stature. However, when combined, as in this room, all of these elements not only state those themes, but push the envelope as they become an exciting treasure chest of excess.

We didn't want to lose the opulent feeling created by the tree, and we felt that the room demanded that the decorations flow from tree to mantle to fireplace and from tabletop to the three French doors. The dark furniture and gold walls made the perfect backdrop for a tree with the look of such great wealth and beauty.

While this house easily supports such a lavish use of black, the color is not so easily incorporated into every home's decor. If you do opt to decorate with black, it is important to have elements in your home to support it; otherwise the look will be jarring and the effect will be uneven and overpowering. But when done correctly, black is simply divine.

▶ **A Hollywood spectacle** Sitting in the living room of a 1920s mansion, this tree shimmers in black, gold, and pearl, and is meant to evoke star style in the early days of silent-screen pictures.

◀ **Garlanded hearth** The dramatic potential of black is given full rein with this magnificent fireplace. Here, a decorative garland was designed to embellish the home's architecture. Lit candles and milk-colored ceramic light bulbs provide a soft glow, reflecting off the golden walls and hearth.

▲ **Reflective glow** By placing some of the ornaments used in this room setting into a bowl, and adding an etched-glass candleholder and several tea lights, this side table was turned into an enticing, glowing display.

◀ **Matched set** The door garlands in this room were all matched to the fireplace, using small- and medium-sized ornaments and black-velvet bows. The garland was lifted in the center to allow the French doors to open easily.

▼ **Draped glamour** Taking advantage of the black metalwork extending down from the stair railing, layered garlands shimmer in the entryway. Ornaments hung from crystal hangers provide shapely, colorful drama.

ROYAL VELVET

Fit for a king and queen, this fifteen-foot-tall tree, set up in the corner of a spacious, ornate drawing room, blends gold with copper to create a medieval feel. Renaissance-inspired shapes and patterns mix with religious icons to evoke the grandeur of cathedrals and royal castles. The crushed-velvet ribbon cascades through the tree like a queen's sash. Matching velvet balls, miniature crowns, and rose-window ornaments produce layers of texture and color, while thin colored-glass icicles add vertical elements reminiscent of the elongated lines of Gothic architecture.

Ornaments of mouth-blown glass painted with eighteen-carat gold help reflect the twinkle of clear miniature lights that illuminate the tree. Under the color-coordinated presents, an oversized tree skirt flows around the tree, evoking a nobleman's cape. The tree's rich tones—traditional bright reds and greens were replaced with deep hunter greens and moody burgundies—add drama to this white, airy space, but may be too dark for a room painted in similarly dusky hues.

▲ **Natural wonder**
The gold, silver, and platinum in this glitter-edged leafy drop offer metallic shine as well as fine craftsmanship, with precise detailing of the leaf veins.

▶ **Royal crown** Ruby beads gather on this inverted teardrop with a decorative gold crown. The ruby is echoed on the tree in other ornaments, and around the room in the velvet ribbons and bows.

▶ **Ornate array** (far right) A strand of dark beaded garland cuts across a grouping of a light fabric ornament and a ball of eighteen-carat gold and clear glass, making a luxurious tapestry of bright and dark, matte and shine.

▲ **Sumptuous garland**
Burgundy and green are repeated in two-tone full-pom bows and beaded garlands in the same colors, accented with a gold cross ornament.

▶ **Velvet jewel box**
This tree is a spectacle of velvet jewel-tones contrasted with the warmth and glitter of polished copper and gold.

JEWEL-TONE GLAMOUR

WHEN MOST PEOPLE THINK OF DECORATING for Christmas, they usually think in terms of traditional colors—primary red and green. Why not dip into other hues of the color palette for something more exotic and dramatic? Royal purple and blue—typically associated with royalty—are traditional colors associated with the Advent season observed by some Christians four weeks before Christmas.

In addition to their religious significance, purple and blue—when combined with vibrant fuchsia, hot orange, golden yellow, ruby red, emerald green, and metallic tones—create a luxurious, festive atmosphere that conjures up a mood of Carnivale, which is famously celebrated the Tuesday before Lent in Venice, Rio de Janeiro, and New Orleans (where it is called Mardi Gras).

Carry the theme throughout your tree with ornaments, bead garland, and ribbon. For a glamorous showstopper of a tree that positively glitters, jewel tones will brighten a dark room, add color to a neutral space, and provide an elegant, different look for a special party.

◀ **Elevated beauty** For a party, a miniature jewel-tone Christmas tree livens up the bar. The multihued ornaments selected for this tree seem even more jewel-like with the addition of color-contrasted glitter in swirl and dot designs. Placing a small tree on a table, bar, or buffet saves space.

▶ **It is best to use a variety** of ornament shapes on your tree—round, elongated, faceted, molded, and angular—and to hang different shapes next to each other whenever possible. Your eyes will be taken on an exciting visual journey. Using ornaments in only one shape creates a static-looking tree.

CROWN JEWEL

The main statement in any Christmas design is always the tree. Therefore, it is important that you choose themed trimmings that will enhance your star attraction. Here, bright Venetian carnival masks and an electric-pink tree skirt intensify the collection of myriad jewel-tone colors. Ribbon was kept to a minimum—just a few swirls of fuchsia-and-gold mesh—so that nothing would detract from the vivid impact of the ornaments. This tree sits in a library window, in front of gauzy burnt-orange curtains, surrounded by curved wooden shelves, leather-bound books, and rich upholstered furniture.

In keeping with the sophisticated surroundings, we used sculpted ornaments. Each ornament was handpainted with intricate designs: lines, arcs, and dots of glitter in contrasting colors. The end result was a lush jewel-like confection that embodied the spirit of Carnivale. Once established in the tree, the party theme was continued throughout the room.

▲ **Sparkling ornaments** Ornaments can be displayed in many ways. If you have ornaments to spare after trimming your tree—and they are beautiful jewels like these—try layering them in wide-rimmed glasses.

▶ **Hot-pink tree skirt** Here we chose a fuchsia tree skirt with faux-marabou feathers and gold-flecked satin; its intense color and material complements the window's burnt-orange satin curtains and the mood of the tree. You could also choose a tree skirt to match any of the other jewel-tones on the tree.

▶ **Etched cocktail glasses** For a party, continue the theme by serving drinks in jewel-colored glasses. Make it more festive with a decorated garland. Or, place a small candle inside each glass to create striking tea lights.

▲ **Statement piece** Present whimsical objects in an upscale way by choosing them in colors or styles that complement your tree. This green rhinestone mask instantly evokes a "Carnivale" feeling.

▶ **Frame your showpiece** A window can frame your main event. The architecture of a home often plays an important part in deciding the location for your tree. An arched doorway or a grand stairway are equally impressive alternatives. Wherever you put it, your tree should always be the center of attention.

A FEAST OF COLORS

Your tree theme can even be introduced into your party menu and buffet decorations. Here, the jewel-tone motif is evident in the dazzling display of rich colors, dramatic textures, fragrant candles, and a sideboard filled with beautiful "jeweled" desserts. The secret to a successful holiday party is to involve your guests. First, make them aware of the party theme. Then encourage them to dress accordingly. Finally, reward them by giving them visually stunning surroundings.

All that is needed to complete this party is atmosphere—a serenading string quartet (or an appropriate CD) to transport us to the romantic canals of Venice and to Carnivale.

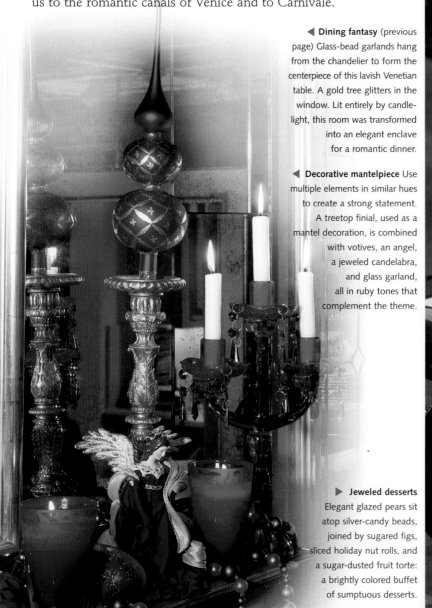

◀ **Dining fantasy** (previous page) Glass-bead garlands hang from the chandelier to form the centerpiece of this lavish Venetian table. A gold tree glitters in the window. Lit entirely by candlelight, this room was transformed into an elegant enclave for a romantic dinner.

◀ **Decorative mantelpiece** Use multiple elements in similar hues to create a strong statement. A treetop finial, used as a mantel decoration, is combined with votives, an angel, a jeweled candelabra, and glass garland, all in ruby tones that complement the theme.

▶ **Jeweled desserts** Elegant glazed pears sit atop silver-candy beads, joined by sugared figs, sliced holiday nut rolls, and a sugar-dusted fruit torte: a brightly colored buffet of sumptuous desserts.

▲ **Feather tree** These brightly colored trees were placed on the table to provide dashes of strong color and a different level to the display. Their sparse, airy design helps showcase a few select ornaments.

▲ **Silverware cozy** Decorative handmade silverware holders provide interesting new twists at the dinner table. Their color-coordinated, luxurious gold design blends well with the overall jewel theme.

▲ **Beads and baubles** Added to the chandelier, multicolored glass beads and brilliant jewel-like ornaments of etched blown glass create additional sparkle as they reflect the gentle glow of candlelight.

Natural Christmas

Y OU CAN BRING THE BEAUTY OF NATURE into your

holiday design, whether you live in the city or the country.

Your trimmings can include flowers, pinecones and berries,

handcrafted ornaments, home-baked goodies, or a combination

of all of these; in natural decorating, individual style is key. This

is probably the most personal of all decorating styles, since the

elements include selecting your favorite flowers, stringing

berries and popcorn, or baking from scratch. We have provided

a range of design ideas, from pastoral to country chic, but the

options are as limitless as nature.

COUNTRY WARMTH

"COUNTRY" IS AN AMBIGUOUS DESCRIPTIVE TERM, because design varies greatly from nation to nation. Whether English Country, American Country, French Country, or Bavarian Country, though, some common elements are shared. Country design has a warm, comfortable feel. Decorations are generally handmade with inexpensive materials found in and around the house. Most have a rural flavor and incorporate elements of nature such as birds, berries, pinecones, and food.

Upscale Country complements modern homes, and is best described as crisp, showcasing pieces like hand-carved wooden decorations made by fine craftspeople. Traditional Country—a natural for rustic homes—is more whimsical and childlike, and features homemade ornaments.

But there are no hard-and-fast rules—although the living room shown here is in a home that is more modern than rustic, we have combined Upscale and Traditional Country elements.

▼ **Bear in the air** This cute collectible hangs high above her fellow cubs, scampering in the tree. Alternating toys, bows, and other special pieces in the garland makes a unique statement.

▲ **Starry night** Red and white balls with painted stars and home-crafted-looking bows add warmth to the tree and garlands. The star motif is echoed in papier-mâché ornaments and the tree lights reflected in the windows like hundreds of twinkling stars.

▶ **Child's play** We designed this display for a family with children. A jolly wooden Santa and snowman placed on either side of the tree fill the space and create a vignette. Clear lights keep the color palette simple. Points of red and green were added to the room with hand-stitched felt stockings and bags, brightly colored ribbon, and a mix of vivid glass ornaments.

COUNTRY CRAFTSMANSHIP

The decorations shown in this living room run the gamut from pieces found in nature to handcrafted decorations with a touch of whimsy to more sophisticated, upscale glass ornaments created by fine craftspeople.

This is not a country-style home, yet we were able to make the mix of country decorations work with the space. So, what do you do if you have a contemporary-looking home but want to decorate it in country style?

First, you remove all of the decidedly "un-country" elements—modern furniture and other pieces in nontraditional colors. For example, in this home, contemporary sculptures were put away for the holiday season. In their places are whimsical decorations in country Christmas colors of red and green, which complement the existing neutral rug and walls.

▶ **Golden pear** An upscale collectible glass piece works with this country setting because of the food motif; the oval shape adds interest and gives a "nod" to the country-fresh egg.

▲ **Snowy sweeper** This ornament also works as a freestanding statement piece. We added him to the fireplace garland to carry on the theme from the tree and to give the whole room a unified look. This decoration is old-fashioned in design and adds a touch of warmth and nostalgia so prominent in country style.

▶ **The "Christmas Pickle"** The glass gherkin hanging here is a tribute to an old German tradition, which dictated that parents were to hide a real pickle in the Christmas tree. The first child to discover the pickle then received an extra gift. This is a fun tradition which families all around the world have adopted and enjoy to this day.

▶ **Felt stocking** (top left) Adding to the homespun feel, this simple handcrafted stocking cheerily enhances the room.

▶ **Painted poinsettia** (top right) This bright green ball with its fiery red flower puts a fresh twist on a traditional image.

▶ **Country sweets** (bottom left) Although real sweets are often used in country Christmas decorating, these donuts, pastries, and stick candies—which appeal to the child in all of us—are glass.

▶ **Sentimental snowman** (bottom right) The use of decorations handed down in the family, like this fabric snowman, gives the tree its nostalgic heart.

◀ **Santa's helper** This cute, red, molded-glass reindeer sports glitter-covered antlers. He, along with other ornaments and felt bags, adds contrast to the brown bears.

▲ **The power of three** At the right end of the fireplace, we placed three different-sized slim-line trees at different heights to form a group that resembles one multilevel tree. Their staggered placement also gives the appearance of trees growing naturally on a hillside.

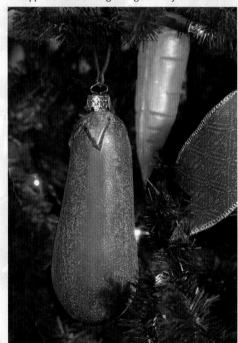

▲ **Shimmering vegetables** The vegetables hung on the fireplace trees are made of molded glass decorated with sparkly glitter, giving these familiar shapes a new slant. They are a fun look for kitchens and dining rooms.

◄ **European country buffet** (previous pages) This home, with its massive stone fireplace, provides a natural setting for a festive dessert buffet surrounded by hints of Europe. Nutcrackers, carved wooden pieces, and the gingerbread-house votive create an inviting atmosphere.

HOLIDAY HEARTH

This room provided interesting challenges. Since the fireplace is made of stone and its contemporary design didn't include a traditional mantelpiece, we were forced to take a different approach to the usual "mantelpiece-decorated-with-garland" look.

We decided to frame the fireplace with freestanding slim-line trees on either side. To create an asymmetrical look, we grouped three trees on one side and placed one large tree alone on the other side. Since the fireplace was not in use, we placed lit holiday greenery in the hearth to brighten the dark space.

▲ **Sugared maple leaves** These holiday "sugar cookie" ornaments bring the dessert theme from table to stairway.

This house sits in a warm climate, but we still wanted to bring the feeling of winter into the home, so we laid a snow blanket at the base of the trees to give them an Alpine flavor. This also echoed the snowy theme on the dining-room table and grounded the look.

▲ **Carved Claus** We attached this two-sided Santa plaque to the stairway banister as a statement piece. The muted colors and antique finish work well with the country theme.

▶ **Simple stairway** A decorative garland hung with statement pieces and stockings makes a nice backdrop to the collection of nutcrackers dressed as characters from *A Christmas Carol* displayed on an adjacent table.

◀ **Holiday harvest** Hung with an array of brightly colored fruits and vegetables and multicolored lights, the main fireplace tree creates a focal point of color in the corner of the dining room.

WINTER FROST

While this tree is perfectly suited to the beamed wood ceilings and inlaid stone floor found in this warm and charming retreat, it would be equally at home in a Swiss mountain chalet or a cozy log cabin. Nostalgic figurines represent images from early-1900s Christmastimes. Whimsical, collectible nutcrackers add Old World charm, while brightly colored cranberry balls and frosted apples and pomegranates give the tree its striking colorful appeal and provide a bright contrast against the frosty white-tipped branches.

Traditional plaid ribbon is woven through the tree, and when combined with pinecones, it makes a nice rustic statement. Ornamental woolen mittens drape over the tree branches as if some playful child just hung them there to dry. Following the line of the ceiling, a decorative garland features antique paper boots, game spinners, balls, and bows. This picturesque setting makes you want to settle into a comfortable chair and wait for the next snowfall while sipping a cup of hot cocoa.

▶ **Bûche de Noël** Originally from France, the *Bûche de Noël*, or yule-log cake, is a perennial holiday favorite that's perfect for a country Christmas. This version has white frosting and is accented with plastic red holly berries.

▲ **Frosted pomegranate** This fruit has long been treasured in the Mediterranean and India for its deep-colored flesh and delicious, winy flavor. This sparkly ruby pomegranate ornament is an excellent addition to country decor.

▶ **Little blue bugle boy** Young boys served as buglers and drummers in the military until the late 19th century, and the bugle-boy motif has persevered. Vintage-style buglers are still popular as ornaments and figurines, and this sweet example fits in perfectly with the rustic theme.

◀ **Santa spinner** Sometimes taking a simple child's toy and placing it in the greenery of the season can add a whimsical tone to the room. This colorful, resin game spinner has an old-time country appeal.

▶ **Snowy charm** Warm woolen mittens, vintage figurines, iced cranberry balls, plaid ribbon, and jeweled pomegranates adorn a sun-dappled, snow-kissed fir. Something this enchanting deserves a stunning finale—a burgundy silk tree skirt, hand-beaded with snowflakes and edged with delicate jingle bells.

AROUND THE FIRE

Who wouldn't want to gather around this warm, inviting hearth, decorated with elements of nature and vintage tableaux set with winter-sledding scenes? The large fireplace allowed for many decorations. In order for this look to work, each piece had to have the feel of both fine craftsmanship and aged beauty. This home is full of stylish yet comfortable furnishings, so we chose a relaxed design to complement the welcoming environment.

Plush stockings hang from the garland, and a wool tree skirt, embellished with hand-beaded snowflakes, lines the table to add an upscale touch of class to the woodsy room. The window is graced with a lit, red-berry wreath that matches the red-berry topiary and ball on the mantelpiece.

Needlepoint pillows with holiday themes accent the couches and the fireplace. A large wooden Santa, driving a reindeer, stands guard in front of a roaring fire, the perfect setting for a family gathering.

▶ **Nature in a jar** (above right) Both real and glass pinecones were used throughout this home; these oil candles filled with pinecones, berries, and evergreen branches brought an extra touch of the outdoors inside.

▶ **Sugared apples and berries** This ball of color works equally well as an ornament or highlight on the mantel of the stone fireplace. Nestled within the frosted branches of the tree, the sugared fruit contributes to the ice-and-snow effect.

▶ **Party on ice** A bevy of bisque-porcelain snow folk frolic on this handpainted votive music box. When it is wound up, a lone skater glides across the pond to the tune of "Jingle Bells."

◀ **Woodland fireplace** Draped from corner to corner with a garland accented with branch twigs and wrapped with patterned ribbon, the fireplace is a multilayered vignette surrounded by lit greenery, candles, and figurines.

▲ **Forest offerings** For a lovely country centerpiece, take a silver bowl, add several pinecone ornaments in muted colors, and highlight with a few autumn-colored glass balls. Place the ensemble in the center of a lit wreath, and surround it with a few decorative candles and figurines.

◀ **Cardinals rule** This brilliantly plumed songbird inhabits woodlands and gardens from eastern Canada to Mexico. The bright red male bird perched here is a common choice in country-Christmas decor because of his cheery appearance.

CHRISTMAS IN BLOOM

NATURE OFFERS A WONDROUS BOUNTY, a colorful array of fresh, fragrant, and visually explosive buds, blooms, and berries. This gorgeous flora, combined with delicate designer glass and a few special accents, bursts into brilliant bloom here as four different geographical areas of the United States are represented by regional floral Christmas trees.

Our design was greatly influenced by which flowers were available in each part of the country. Therefore, for these unique trees, we chose to decorate with flowers, fruits, and plants that were available and popular regionally, and to showcase these elements in ways not commonly envisioned—such as mixing ice twigs with orchids or limes with pinecones to create a dramatic artistic statement. The element common to all four designs was the artificial-tree base, yet each tree was given an individual personality by customizing the trimmings.

◀ **Radiant and vibrant** (clockwise from top left) Miniature New Zealand calla lilies adorn the Northeastern tree, coxcomb and hypericum berries populate the Midwestern tree, waxflowers and roses inhabit the Southern vignette, and eggplant, protea, and kale mingle in the Western display.

◀ **Rosy delight** Not wanting to detract from the floral theme, for the Southern tree we chose designer pieces with handpainted flowers instead of plain glass balls. A dainty rose dangles below this ball, enhancing the flowery mood.

▲ **Stately sunflowers** An intricate seed pattern, framed by bold orange and lemony yellow rays, makes sunflowers a beautiful addition to floral displays. These glittery glass examples, used in the Western tree, stand out when mixed in with live flowers.

◀ **Romantic arrangement** Juniper and cedar branches, waxflowers, and roses spill forth from this distressed cast-iron urn from Paris. We included live flowers to add both intoxicating fragrance and natural beauty to the Southern tree.

NORTHEAST CHIC

The Northeast is represented with a dazzling display of orchids and roses that enhances this light-filled bedroom. The crowning touch is a spectacular treetop, created by Donald Clay, which merges live orchids with icy twigs made from crushed safety-glass attached to tree branches with glue (available at floral-supply stores). They make a nice contrast to each other, suggesting the crispness of winter and the promise of spring.

Green pears, arranged on the desk and inserted in the tree, create a through-line (a design element that ties a look together) in this room, and they echo the color of the orchids. Bright red was introduced to the tree sparingly by hanging glass balls that beautifully set off the green pears and orchids. To add to this tree's unique look, we included upside-down silver vases filled with floral accents.

▲ **Bouquets of roses and lilies** An heirloom sterling-silver tea set lends classy support to the overall design. You can use everyday items found throughout the house as accent pieces.

◀ **Bedroom romance** Bright red rose petals scattered generously on the bedspread contrast with the deep greens of the tree and bed covering—and they also add a dramatic expression of passion.

▼ **Floral treasure** This glass piece is both an ornament and a "pick" (a decorative branch-tip accessory). It easily clips onto tree branches, garlands, and wreaths. Position it carefully so it stands up straight.

◀ **Cool and crisp** The tree is draped with acrylic "ice-chip" garlands and icy twigs interspersed with large crystal snowflake ornaments, recreating the icy feel of a Northeast winter's day.

▲ **Lilies on ice** The calla lily thrives in greenhouses all over the world. While most popular as an Easter decoration, it looks equally lovely at Christmas displayed in a clear vase filled with glass "ice."

MIDWEST HARVEST

Pinecones are the main feature of the Midwestern tree; we selected them for their traditional, homey feeling. This feeling was echoed in the cranberry and popcorn garlands that were meticulously handstrung, piece by piece. A tradition carried over from Victorian times, the craft of stringing fruits and other foods is time-consuming. There are prefabricated reproductions available on the market, but they cannot substitute for the fun of making garlands with friends and family.

Native Midwestern fruits and plants such as juniper, rosemary, and crabapples are clustered together throughout the tree and garland, making colorful statement pieces. Freshly sliced limes add a decorative twist. Fuchsia-colored coxcomb, with its fuzzy, textured surface, brings in warm luxury. The waxy-looking surface of the hypericum (also called coffee berry) provides a gentle reflection of light, and the delicate miniature yellow and red spray roses counterbalance the sharp-edged cedar and juniper branches. The finishing touch: large floral ornaments in traditional red and green.

▶ **Nutcracker tassel** This clever decoration was made by attaching the top half of a miniature carved wooden nutcracker to a bunch of colorful threads; the end result is a stylish tassel ornament.

◀ **Harvest beauty** Strings of popcorn and cranberries create irregular and eye-catching lines across this country-style tree. Clusters of sliced and whole fruit, inviting florals, and pinecones in various sizes—from small to enormous—convey an earthy heartland mood.

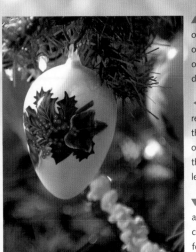

▲ **Holiday craft** By taking a single ornament and combining it with a handful of berries, a few flowers, and a short piece of live or artificial ivy, you can create a decorative accent for your window.

◀ **Holly and ivy** The contrast of the red berries, deep, dark green ivy, and the serrated edges of the holly stand out on this white egg-shaped ornament that echoes the clusters of fruit and leaves elsewhere on the tree.

▼ **Santa's ride** This tabletop floral arrangement, arranged tightly in a sleigh, contains all of the floral and fruity elements found on the tree. Its cheery countenance brightens the room and expands the theme.

WESTERN CORNUCOPIA

The Western wilderness was the inspiration for this tree. We carefully placed branches and other elements in the tree to give an illusion of natural randomness. As in the other floral trees, roses played a part in our decorating scheme, providing many bright points of color in sharp contrast to the dark green of the tree and branches. They also softened the look.

A touch of the exotic was added by introducing bright orange birds of paradise (which grow freely throughout the Western states) and deep-crimson pomegranates. Sliced oranges contributed a fragrant citrus appeal. For novelty's sake, we replaced the traditional tree stand with an antique apple pail. Once again, glass ornaments were kept to a minimum, except for those that worked well with the Western floral theme in both color and design.

▶ **Red, red rose** Handpainted ornaments such as this rose ball help to continue the rose theme, prevalent in all four floral displays in this chapter. Roses are readily available in all parts of the country.

▲ **Exotic bouquet** This eclectic grouping of sliced citrus, pinecones, and assorted flowers creates an exciting cluster. Place bunches like this throughout your tree and on garlands, or use them to enhance tabletop topiaries.

▼ **Glittery florals** This unusual piece helps to bring a feeling of lightness and glitter to an otherwise dark and heavy tree. Its warm colors complement the tree and room tones.

◀ **Wild West** This wild tree looks perfectly at home in its cottage-like environment. The relaxed design was inspired by the informal gardens surrounding this home.

▲ **Bucket bouquet** To create a rough, rural country feeling, a rustic metal bucket was filled with colorful roses arranged around a red-and-green apple center.

SOUTHERN ELEGANCE

This tree personifies classic Southern romance. In creating it, we were inspired by imagery from the works of Southern authors such as Margaret Mitchell, Mark Twain, and Anne Rice. Fragrant magnolia blossoms, salmon-pink roses, and drippy Spanish moss conjured up visions of the old South and days of gracious living in simpler times. The Southern look works especially well in rooms that are decorated with casual floral patterns and painted in muted or neutral colors.

Traditional red and green Christmas elements just wouldn't work with this particular theme. Instead, we used a small number of handpainted, floral-themed ornaments in a variety of styles, shapes, and colors. Tree branches and mosses create interesting lines and textures. Roses and waxberries in pastel shades expand on the enchanting floral theme.

◀ **Matched set** A decorative glass handbag and shoe have feminine Southern charm and keep the tree dressed in style.

▶ **Summer breeze** This sultry, romantic tree entices; a gentle wind seems to waft through the branches, while the flowers bloom and release perfume into the air. Flowers fill different-sized urns and props placed at varying heights, creating a multilevel garden.

▼ **Pussywillows and poppies** Delicate depictions of flowers, in the form of glass ornaments with handpainted blossoms and branches, help to accentuate the "ladies-who-lunch" feel of the tree.

▲ **Flower garden** Framed by amaranthus to the left and magnolia leaves to the right, this gold, red, green, and white ornament brings all the colors found on the tree onto one glass canvas.

▶ **Lovers entwined** Passionate pink roses sit nestled in an aluminum watering can, in the embrace of a sturdy tree branch—a delicate dance between the masculine arms of the tree and the feminine softness of the roses.

Pop Culture

ECLECTIC, ALTERNATIVE, TRENDY, FUN: these styles all
allow for total freedom of expression. They follow no rules of
design. Whether you are looking back to your childhood for
inspiration, creating an amazing party surprise for your guests, or
just showcasing your collectibles, the bottom line is to cut loose . . .
anything goes! Use your imagination and "think outside the box."

RETRO WHIMSY

RETRO IS JUST ANOTHER WORD for nostalgia. In the 1950s, oversized, multicolored light bulbs (C-9s), tinsel icicles, and large, colorful glass ornaments defined the look of a Christmas tree. Before the advent of themed trees and designer ornaments, Christmas trees incorporated a variety of traditional elements representative of Christmas: Santas, elves, candy canes, train sets, and gift-wrapped packages stacked under the tree.

What once stood as the standard for Christmas is now just one of many choices in the broad spectrum of holiday themes and designs. Like Victorian, this design is specific to one particular era, but its appeal is timeless.

◄ **Gingerbread man** To make a cookie decoration, poke a hole into the cookie before it fully cools to prevent breakage. Once the cookie cools, ice it and thread a piece of floral wire through the hole and hang.

◄ **Helping-hands kitchen** Gingerbread cookies serve two purposes: they are tasty holiday treats as well as holiday decorations. A whimsical Christmas village built on a buffet adds to the warmth of the kitchen and pulls your eye toward the Christmas display in the adjacent room. A needlepoint potato-chip-canister Santa smiles in approval.

▲ **Jaunty cap** A novelty light cap in the shape of Santa's hat is perfect for a retro setting. The hat sits over a simple miniature bulb. Mix novelty light sets with plain lights to prevent your design from looking too busy.

◄ **Combined charm** This clever snow-globe plays music and has a built-in candle to light the way for Santa and his reindeer as they revolve around the base. In the background, his final destination: a quaint, snowy illuminated village.

A CHILD'S PARTY

Create a festive environment for your child (or the child in you) by removing all things adult and everyday. This clears your decorating space and allows you to build a Christmas fantasy land. In this particular home, it was the dining room that was transformed from an ordinary workspace into a place filled with wonder and visual excitement.

The goal was to design something fanciful, suitable for a child's Christmas lunch. We mixed primary colors with traditional Christmas reds and greens to achieve a bright, fun palette reminiscent of a box of crayons.

On the table, felt ornaments in shapes ranging from snowmen and Santas to angels and gift packages double as silverware pockets. Even the milk glasses got a holiday makeover: each base has its own slip-on "skirt" with decorative appliqués. Peppermint candles burn and scent the air with their gentle aroma, and small decorative items scattered about the table lend their charms.

▶ **Fun with felt** This perky snowman with his bright-red scarf and cheery smile has become a Christmas staple. He evokes memories of childhood arts-and-crafts projects created around the kitchen table.

▶ **Bag of sweets** This brightly colored felt bag hangs merrily on the tree. Inside, candy canes and assorted sweets await a child's eager hand on Christmas morning.

◀ **Holiday hutch** Deck out your dining-room furniture by removing everyday dishes and filling the nooks and crannies with everything Christmas. Turn an ordinary hutch into an exciting showcase for all your Christmas collectibles, dishes, and figurines.

▲ **Gingerbread house** This sweet edifice dominates the Christmas table. It sits atop a vintage ceramic holiday decoration and is accented with artificial snow.

▼ **Cookies and milk** Frosted Christmas cookies, a glass of milk, and a colorful place setting await the arrival of each child at a playful holiday lunch.

AROUND THE TREE

This is where it all happens on Christmas morning, as colorful lights brighten the room and the sound of the train whistle cuts through the air. Children and adults alike descend on the piles of brightly wrapped presents, eagerly anticipating what's inside. The crowning moment when the wait is over has at last arrived—Christmas is finally here!

In order to create treasured memories like these, first make sure that your tree sits in an accessible location. If children are involved, include them by making decorations together and then hanging your decorations on the tree. The nostalgic look shown here is about family and remembering the past, and is inspired by Christmas days long gone.

Keeping family decorations and placing them on the tree from year to year helps to keep memories and traditions alive. You can buy collectible ornaments, but sometimes the ones that are the most valuable are those that you make yourself.

▲ **Tool-time elf** A vintage elf—one of Santa's rosy-cheeked toymakers—is surrounded by tools from his workshop: a gaily painted glass wrench and screwdriver.

◀ **Childhood memory** This tree is considered by many to be the definitive look of Christmas, with its brightly colored lights and fabulous tinsel icicles.

▶ **Fire engine** Many a child has wished for a shiny fire truck on Christmas. This glass ornament is a nod to those dreams.

▼ **Chugging along** Train sets bring back memories of hours spent playing in imaginary towns under the trees of our youth.

◀ **Stained-glass Santa** This crystal-like Kringle would normally be hung in a window to take advantage of direct sunlight. For something different, try incorporating window decorations into the tree.

▲ **Plucky ducky** This cheery pull-toy is right at home on this tree filled with childhood enchantments. Simple white buttons are the wheels on a cart, made to steer this yellow fellow about.

LOOKING IN

The retro style is known as much for the decorations displayed outside the home as for those inside. A classic retro home leaves no dark area untouched. Every single available space is filled with lit plastic figures, large multicolored ceramic light bulbs, decorative wreaths and garlands, animated pieces, and a candelabra in every window.

Homes are decked out from ground to roof. Santa, flying with his eight tiny reindeer, frequently takes a break from his hectic delivery schedule on Christmas Eve to stop by for a guest appearance and wave from the rooftop.

◄ **White magic** Multicolored bubble lights stand out dramatically against this white tree, sitting in front of a darkened window. Stained-glass holiday figures and decorative glass plates make fashionable accessories.

► **Berry wreath** Illuminated with tiny clear lights, this circle of berries makes for a warm welcome on the front door.

▲ **Snowy carolers** Lighting up to greet holiday visitors, snowman bulbs put on happy faces and help set the festive mood.

◄ **Debi's vintage Claus** This plastic Santa head has stood the test of time. It hung on Debi's childhood home in New Jersey, but migrated west to new California digs.

▼ **Bob's sentinels** Framed by strings of multicolored lights and oversized novelty bulbs in front of the patio, two toy soldiers stand guard. They date back to Bob's youth; recently relocated from Michigan to Hollywood, they arrived in time for their big break.

SMALL QUARTERS

Decorating a more intimate space, such as a condo or cottage, works on the same principles as decorating a large house, just on a smaller scale. Living in an apartment should not diminish your holiday spirit. Since you have a smaller area to decorate, make your holiday display count. Select a few fine pieces and feature them prominently, rather than using many smaller, less impactful decorations.

You should always start your design with the largest element, which in most cases will be the Christmas tree. Depending on the space available, you may want to use a small tree and set it on a table to give the illusion of greater height, or try a slimline tree, which is tall and narrow.

Most apartments do not have working fireplaces, so if you like to use garland, you can drape it over large pieces of furniture, frame a mirror, outline a window, or run it along your holiday buffet.

▶ **Live retro** This tree mixes upscale glass ornaments with traditional vintage decorations. In lieu of a tree skirt, white cotton batting was placed at the base of the tree. On the coffee table, a train-depot vignette also sits on a bed of cotton "snow."

▶ **European angel** Surrounded by delicate gossamer strands of spun gold, this angel looks heavenly.

▲ **Red ball** This is an upscale reproduction of a classic retro design. With its intricate molded glass shape, including an additional ball at the bottom, lovely glitter pattern, and vibrant color, it stands out and makes a fine collectible.

▶ **Sock monkey** Hanging from a branch and clutching a banana, a cute glass monkey ornament provides comic relief. In true retro fashion, this tree combines sophisticated designer pieces with whimsical elements.

▲ **Snow angel** This brightly clad little boy has happily plopped down in the snow and eagerly waves his arms and legs to create the outline of an angel.

◀ **Roly-poly snowman** Another playful piece on this retro tree is the well-coordinated snowman here, outfitted in matching hat, scarf, and mittens and carrying a broom to help clear a path in the snow.

TROPICAL DELIGHT

WARM CLIMATES INSPIRE alternative holiday decorations. Located inside a poolside guesthouse, this tree can be used in some parts of the country year-round. It is the ultimate cool party prop.

In recent years, the tropical theme has island-hopped to the mainland and gained greater acceptance. Surfing Santas, tropical fruits, and exotic flowers have freed many decorators from what has long been considered the conventional and only correct way to decorate the home for Christmas.

This tropical tree is a classic example of decorating according to the style of the house. Eschewing the traditional treetop, we set aside the artificial tree's actual top and made use of this guesthouse living room's rattan palm-tree chandelier instead.

▶ **Exotic cocktails** Green-cactus glasses serve up freshly sliced limes along with an explosion of tropical glass ornaments—pineapples, sugared conch shells in pretty pastels, vivid bird-of-paradise blooms, and shy seahorses—turning a simple bar decoration into an island stunner.

◀ **Fruit medley** Keeping it light and fruity, this garland plays host to a variety of sweet, tropical delights. Fresh limes, blown-glass pineapples and watermelon slices, and paper strawberries and pears create a mouthwatering fruit salad.

▶ **Poolside party** This shows how you can take one simple, inexpensive, and offbeat element and turn it into an entire tree. Several hundred cocktail umbrellas serve as bright, tropical bursts of color on a tree grounded with lime-green packing peanuts! Hawaiian-themed designer ornaments add special island flavor.

ISLAND FLAVOR

Christmas ornaments shaped like rainbow-hued fish, unusual local flowers, and brightly plumed birds evoke daydreams of vacations on exotic islands around the world.

A tropical tree sets the scene for a party—in your house, at poolside, along the ocean, or in your own personal backyard paradise. Make your tree the life and soul of the party. This bright beacon of light and form can be used to provide unique and alternative lighting as your party changes from a sunny afternoon barbecue into a late-evening luau.

The placement of the tree is vitally important when used as a party prop. Decide whether you want to use it to draw guests into your soiree, to point the way to the bar or buffet or, as seen here, to stand alone—apart from the party—and merely cast a lovely reflection into the pool.

Remember: As with all things electrical, be sure to keep cords and lights well away from the water. Extension cords should be secured. (Safety should always be part of holiday festivities!)

▶ **Dazzling flier** A Native American myth tells how the first two hummingbirds were created from feathers left over from other birds. The sun cast rays on the pair, causing the male to glow with brilliant colors. This clip-on fellow is caught midflight.

▲ **Snorkelers' treasure** The guesthouse tree on the previous page was decorated with a multitude of tropical fauna ornaments; this one is inspired by the Moorish Idol reef fish. The Hawaiian name for the fish is *kihi kihi,* meaning "angular," a reference to its shape—which offers a nice contrast to the round cocktail umbrellas.

▶ **Tropical tranquility** This limited-edition collectible, titled "Paradise," depicts a white ship floating through an idyllic ocean sunset. What makes it unique are the raised flowers and leafy palm-tree fronds circling the ornament.

◀ **Island sunset** A Hawaiian-shirt ornament is handpainted with a rippling sea, swaying palms, and a distant volcano that hint at warm breezes and romantic nights.

▶ **Ribbons of light** Here, we used electric ribbon as an alternative to traditional Christmas tree lights—it is weather-resistant and safe for outdoor use. The tropical colors make it perfect for a poolside party. The potted flowers below serve two purposes: to secure the tree and to provide a decorative tree-stand cover.

ALTERNATIVE STYLE

SANTA CLAUS, RUDOLPH, and red and green are left behind, as nontraditional colors and ornaments replace them in holiday decorating. Tired of your green tree? Substitute hot pink, purple, or black. Hang your tree off the ceiling, replace ornaments with designer photographs and bath accessories, or create a theme with anything—including the bathroom sink!

This style of decorating is for all the unconventional freethinkers out there, those people who want a change from Santa and Frosty. No Dasher, no Dancer, nor Prancer, nor Vixen here. This is the land of zebras and leopards and the Society of Red Hats. The Eiffel Tower, the Hollywood sign, and a double-decker bus from London stand in for toy-making elves and Santa's flying sleigh. So, find the rebel in you and do something wild!

▶ **Ornamental scrubbie** In keeping with the fun, whimsical atmosphere of this spectacularly decorated bathroom, pink bath scrubbies were turned into flowery "ornaments."

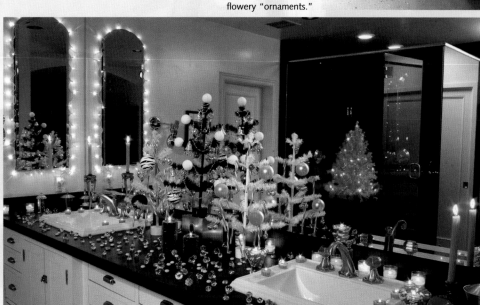

◀ **Reflecting pool** Party guests will delight in this festive use of the bathtub. Lit candles of many different sizes and shapes fill and surround a common bathtub and transform it into a reflective pool of light.

▲ **Fantasy vanity** Candies and crystals give this ordinary bathroom countertop a chance to sparkle. Pink candy canes hang from pink, white, and black feather trees. Miniature tea lights give the room a rosy glow.

FASHION COLORS

Hot pink, black, passion purple, teal, yellow, and white
are not color choices normally associated with the typical,
everyday Christmas tree. If you are looking to decorate
"outside the box" in a fun and funky way, try a tree in a
nontraditional color. These alternative colors work well
when used to set a mood or create a specific atmosphere.
They look best when displayed in contemporary settings,
making use of unusual locations.

Are you throwing a wild party? Are you interested in
creating a conversation piece that your guests will talk about
for years to come? Try placing your colorful creation in an
unexpected place—like in a shower stall, in the middle of a
pool, or hanging upside-down over your dining-room table
to stand in as a holiday chandelier. If you have a white living
room, try a black tree hung with black-and-white photographs
to lend an air of sophistication and elegance.

▲ **Crystal copycats** This clear acrylic
snowflake and glass-beaded wire heart
replicate the look of fine crystal. They
act as brilliant jewels on this black tree.

▶ **Smoke and sparkle** We chose this
ornament to match the black-and-white
photographs prominently displayed on
the tree. Silver leaves add glitter.

◀ **Wet and wild shower** The bathroom-
party theme from the previous page
culminates in a hot-pink tree with glass
"soap bubbles," accented with bath
accessories and lit candles. Use outdoor
lights; keep all cords away from water.

▲ **Photo gallery** This
tree is a perfect example
of how you can use one
or more images to
create your very own
photographic exhibit
for Christmas.

◀ **Lily in black-and-
white** An elegant print
by Edie Baskin-Bronson,
acclaimed for her
Saturday Night Live
portrait photography,
serves as a simple, stylish
statement piece.

▶ **Travel treasures** Large, lit buildings are heavy statement pieces and require strong branches for support, so we used an artificial tree.

TRAVELER'S TREE

Your Christmas tree can be a perfect setting for all those collectibles and souvenirs gathered on your travels. Instead of placing your lit-house collection either under the tree or on a nearby table, make the buildings focal points on your tree. Here, pieces such as the Empire State Building and Radio City Music Hall were carefully wired into the tree. We added faux snow to provide separation between pieces, enabling you to see everything on display. The ornaments were collected from around the world. What better way to showcase an Egyptian pharaoh, the Hollywood sign, and a Turkish slipper than on your own personalized Christmas tree? We enhanced the nearby window with star lights, a Santa nutcracker, colorful finials, and a glass tree-shaped plate.

▲ **Egg art** A handcrafted egg created by a local tribe in the hills of Mexico provides a burst of color as well as fond memories.

▲ **Experience New York** A city taxicab and a famous landmark come together here. Try grouping related collectibles in your design.

TOPSY-TURVY

There are several different reasons you might choose to use an upside-down tree. Many retailers use an upside-down tree because it shows off decorations better, since they hang out of the tree and aren't obscured by branches. It also creates an unusual, eye-catching floor display. Collectors like this tree because it shows off their valued treasures to best advantage.

Another great reason to use this particular tree is that it takes up a minimum of floor space while providing the same amount of display area as a regular Christmas tree. Best of all, it looks cool and there is a lot more room for presents!

This tree needs to be attached to the ceiling in multiple locations with monofilament (fishing line) that is either tied around beams or tied to screws that have been drilled into ceiling joists. It also should be anchored properly at its base, using sandbags or something similarly heavy.

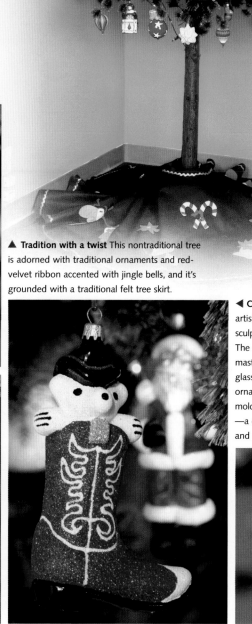

▲ **Tradition with a twist** This nontraditional tree is adorned with traditional ornaments and red-velvet ribbon accented with jingle bells, and it's grounded with a traditional felt tree skirt.

▲ **Holiday express** When using a collectible set that tells a story, it is important to hang them together in logical display order—like this molded-glass train set, which we hung in a straight line.

▶ **Up, up, and away!** This brightly colored hot-air balloon looks like it is floating through the air when suspended from the branches of our inverted Christmas tree.

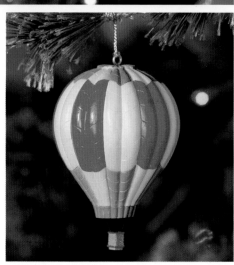

◀ **Covered in glitter** The Chicago artist who created these two pieces sculpted each design out of clay. The sculptures were then made into master molds and filled with molten glass. After cooling, the glass ornaments were removed from the molds and glittered. The final results —a cute bear in a cowboy boot and a merry gingerbread man. ▼

STORYTELLING

Themed trees are another way of telling a story. You can design Christmas trees around books, favorite films, memorable experiences, or holidays. If you are a collector of hats, showcase them! Grandma's wedding dress makes a great romantic statement in a tree. Or, if you are a lover of animals, have fun with a design depicting endangered species or favorite breeds of cats or dogs—or design a tree dedicated to your own pet using photos and pet treats.

The size of your "story" will dictate the size of your tree. If you are planning on telling the story of the birth of civilization, you will need a very large tree! Joking aside, start thinking about your design by laying out the pieces you want to spotlight; then determine how big a tree you need to display your chosen decorations. Decide whether you would like to use a traditional green tree or something snazzier. Look for other pieces that will complement or add to your story. This can be done with color, ribbon, fabric, and other objects or ornaments. A decorative tree skirt makes a perfect ending for your story. The main goal is to have fun, be creative, and enjoy your collectibles.

▶ **The Red Hat Society** There is an international society of ladies who get together, wear red hats and purple dresses, do wild and crazy things, and just flat-out enjoy themselves. The only catch is that you have to be of a certain age to join. This tree is fondly dedicated to all those wild women. It captures their carefree spirit, sense of fun, and red-hat style.

◀ **Haunted holiday** Since people collect ornaments for various holidays, a great way to show them off is to create a small tabletop display dedicated to holiday themes. Then the decorations can be changed from holiday to holiday. Orange, purple, and green satin provide a colorful base for this spooky tribute to Halloween. The Victorian tree stand adds to the moodiness.

▲ **Wildlife treasures** A hot-pink tree serves as the palette for these sophisticated, collectible animal heads in shades of black-and-white. Faux-leopard ribbon gives the tree added texture and dimension, while silver stars provide glitter. This tree was dramatic enough on its own, so we didn't use lights.

◀ **Bridal memories** A vintage wedding gown is this tree's statement piece. It is the perfect tree for a Christmas wedding, if the bride wants to include her mother's —or grandmother's —beautiful gown in the ceremony. The tree is hung with pearl garlands and gold and white ornaments, and finished with a regal embroidered-satin tree skirt.

Debi's Celebrity Ornaments

Since moving to Hollywood, I've had numerous opportunities to collect celebrity autographs. I "stole" Bob's idea of having ornaments signed, but I tried to select ornaments that I felt suited each individual signer's personality. As you can see, this has made for quite an eclectic ornament collection.

1. Michael York / Mindy Sterling
2. Tracey Ullman 3. Jay Leno
4. Tai Babilonia 5. Majel Barrett
6. Jack Lemmon 7. Smokey
Robinson 8. Whoopi Goldberg
9. Mickey Rooney 10. Julie Andrews /
Blake Edwards 11. Wesley Snipes
12. Cindy Williams 13. Jon Cryer
14. Billy Crystal 15. Jack Paar
16. Steve Allen 17. RuPaul
18. Jillian Barberie 19. Peri Gilpin /
Christian Vincent 20. Victor Alfieri /
Peter Reckell / Kristian Alfonso /
Joe Mascolo (Days of Our Lives)
21. Christopher Radko 22. Tom
Leykis 23. Tim Conway / Harvey
Korman / Carol Burnett (Carol
Burnett Show) 24. Louie Anderson
25. Betty Garrett 26. Phyllis George
27. Jason Alexander 28. Bronson
Pinchot 29. Yvonne Craig
30. Don Adams 31. Jerry Maren
32. Peter Tomarken 33. Michael
Ansara 34. Dave Prowse
35. Stephen Collins 36. Walter
Koenig 37. Jerry Springer
38. Connie Stevens 39. LeVar Burton
40. Dr. Joyce Brothers 41. Martin
Mull 42. Vikki Carr 43. Michael
Cimino 44. Johnny Brown
45. Tom Bergeron 46. Frank
Gorshin 47. Valerie Perrine
48. Bruce Jenner 49. Richard
Grieco 50. Jane Withers
51. Sam Rubin 52. Jackie Collins
53. Teri Garr 54. George Clooney
55. Tammy Faye 56. Ken Osmond
57. Lisa Loring / Ken Weatherwax
(The Addams Family) 58. Bret
Saberhagen 59. Markie Post
60. Joey Heatherton 61. Rita Rudner
62. Adam West 63. Rod Taylor
64. Al Michaels 65. Deidre Hall
66. Dorothy Lucey 67. Robin
Williams 68. Bobcat Goldthwait
69. Marta Kristen / Angela
Cartwright / June Lockhart / Bill
Mumy / Bob May (Lost in Space)
70. Candy Clark 71. David Selby

2

THE 12 DAMES OF CHRISTMAS

've always loved the expression "What a dame," especially when it was uttered by some he-man type in those fabulous old movies I used to watch as a kid. I understood that the men never meant the word *dame* as an insult, but as a sign of respect. They recognized dames as strong women who were unwilling to be pushed into the background. I also loved that you always knew when a dame entered the room, and you also knew when she left.

But why dedicate an entire section to the great dames of film and stage in a book about Christmas? I could answer that "The 12 Dames of Christmas" makes for a great play on words (you know it does). I could give you a long-winded designer-type speech about concepts and creative expression (blah, blah, blah). But I won't. The simple truth is that these women should be talked about and remembered. Yes, even at Christmas.

Also, how often is a designer privileged enough to work with authentic costumes and vintage movie props? I had this rare and happy opportunity thanks to The Hollywood History Museum in the Historic Max Factor Building, the Alex Theatre, and History for Hire, all in Los Angeles.

This is just another way of looking at Christmas-tree design. While you probably wouldn't recreate any of the trees shown here, what you could do is feature your own private favorite celebrity on a tree, using pictures, CDs, album covers, or any other relevant (or irreverent) ephemera.

All of the following women were chosen for their larger-than-life personas, the sense of "WOW" that they bring to the world, and most of all, their ability to survive it all. My only regret is that there wasn't enough space to include more of the ladies. In my defense, I can only say that if you enjoy looking at the Dames as much as I enjoyed recreating them, then there will be books including even more of your favorites in the future. Remember, in Hollywood, if it's a hit, there's gotta be a sequel!

ELIZABETH TAYLOR

—— Cinema's Queen of the Nile ——

SHE HAS BEEN CALLED "the last movie star" and the most beautiful woman in the world. Women have envied her, and men have sought her favors even if it meant personal ruin. So what better choice to portray Egypt's legendary Queen of the Nile in the 1963 movie *Cleopatra* than Elizabeth Taylor?

The role of Cleopatra was an obvious one for the actress, who at that time was at her cinematic peak. Cleopatra was considered by the ancients to be a woman of great power and beauty, a woman who almost toppled ancient Rome. The irony was not lost on Hollywood when the film became a financial disaster and nearly toppled 20th Century Fox.

But unlike the ill-fated Egyptian queen, Elizabeth Taylor survived and went on to play her greatest role: that of human-rights activist.

My goal as a designer was to find the perfect setting that would honor each woman's grand legacy. Under the cobalt-blue ceiling of the historic Alex Theatre in Glendale, California, I found it.

◀ **Egyptian splendor** The tree is a tribute to Hollywood's version of ancient Egypt: the grand epic *Cleopatra*. The glittering gold and cobalt-blue ornaments are informed by Egyptian imagery: pyramids, gods, pharaohs, and queens.

▶ **Beautiful rulers** Queen Nefertiti, like Cleopatra, was a strong woman whose beauty was legendary, but she ruled as well as any man—with strength and cunning. This ornament was based on the famous bust on display at the Berlin Museum.

◀ **Floating down the Nile** This royal Egyptian barge provides a different shape for the tree, as opposed to the standard, round Christmas ball. Unusual pieces like this support the tree theme in 3-D. The sail is painted with the Eye of Horus, a symbol for the Egyptian falcon-headed sun god.

JOAN CRAWFORD

——— Hollywood's Cinderella ———

NO ONE COULD DENY that Joan Crawford was a star of the first order. She was a strong-willed woman and a dedicated actress who crafted and guarded her public image as if it was her sole purpose for living. Throughout her career—which spanned over 50 years—Joan Crawford played many roles, but many considered her greatest role ever to be that of Joan Crawford, "star."

Since Joan loved being a star and knew the value of good publicity, I placed her tree in the glamorous Art Deco lobby of the Historic Max Factor building, located in the heart of Hollywood, California. It was here that makeup and hair stylist extraordinaire Max Factor helped transform the Texan chorus girl Lucille Fay LeSueur into Joan Crawford.

In fact, he performed such a startling transformation that forever after Joan was known as MGM's Cinderella. Women around the world followed her life, copied her style, and eagerly anticipated her next fashion move. Her face, vanity, and fashion sense helped to make her famous, but it was her artistry, technical proficiency, and ability to adapt to change that kept her a star and made her a legend.

◀ **From duckling to swan** The swan ornament irresistibly parallels the fabled story of an ugly duckling turned swan and the transformation of the unpolished Lucille Fay LeSueur into the elegant Joan Crawford.

▼ **Fairytale coach** What better symbol than this to represent Joan's new life as young Hollywood royalty? The sparkling white, pink, and gold coach adds a whimsical element to this Cinderella story.

◀ **Beauty shot** The tree was composed like one of Joan's glamorous Hollywood studio portraits of the '30s and '40s; it reposes slightly, draped in satin, with an upturned "face" illuminated by strong, dramatic light.

LANA TURNER
— One Cool Beauty —

MGM's sultry "Sweater Girl" Lana Turner frequently appeared in shadow in film noir pictures such as *The Postman Always Rings Twice*, and she often portrayed women with shady pasts.

I designed this tree with an emphasis on black-and-white because that's how I always pictured her. She was a creature I never associated with color.

The tree was shot in Max Factor's blue "For Blondes Only" room, where he did hair and makeup for Hollywood's blond leading ladies. Blue represents the flashing neon signs and cold shadows in the backwater bars that Lana's characters often inhabited. Blue also stands for her icy beauty.

Matching sets Lana's tree is as glamorous as she was. Everything is coordinated—from her dress, purse, and hatboxes to the ornaments and tree fabric. Lana Turner's bad girls always had killer style.

Compact style A tool in any femme fatale's arsenal, her compact kept Lana looking her best. It also allowed her to look over her shoulder!

MARILYN MONROE

— Sweet Confection —

MARILYN MONROE is perhaps the most famous woman of the 20th century. Because of the myths surrounding her, I could never get a good sense of who she was. In fact, nobody ever seemed to get to know the real Marilyn.

She was always just out of reach to me, and in order to create this tree I knew I needed an inspiration, some kind of connection to her. That connection came to me at a county fair. I watched an older gentleman take ordinary sugar and red food dye and pour it into a large machine. The machine began to spin these common elements into something light, beautiful, and tastier than it was before. Then I thought, "This is what the Hollywood machine did to Norma Jean Baker. It made her into a cotton-candy confection called Marilyn Monroe."

◄ **Light as air** Celebrity photographer Milton H. Greene forever immortalized Marilyn Monroe in his 1955 photos of her wrapped in white fur. Here, Marilyn's glamorous fur wraps not only around her, but around the entire tree, in a room as airy as cotton candy.

▲ **Pretty in pink** In keeping with the theme of Marilyn's tree, this egg-shaped ornament appears to be delicately sprinkled with pink-tinted sugar crystals.

LUCILLE BALL

For Redheads Only

WHEN I THINK OF LUCILLE BALL, I see the movie star who was always glimmering just below her greatest creation, Lucy Ricardo. On those rare moments when the *I Love Lucy* scripts allowed her out of her 1950s housedresses, Lucille the movie star shone through. Many people confused Lucy Ricardo with Lucille Ball the actress. But long before *I Love Lucy*, there was a film career that introduced us to young Lucille's comedic ability and showed us that she was much more than just a beautiful redhead.

In fact, Lucille was born a brunette, arrived in Hollywood a blonde, and was transformed by Max Factor into the zany redhead we all know and love.

I placed Lucille's tree in Max Factor's "For Redheads Only" room, which was designed in complementary shades of green with her specifically in mind. I chose to present her as Lucille the movie star at her dressing table, not Lucy the comedienne, to remind the world that Lucille had a film career both before and after *I Love Lucy*.

▶ **Green inspiration** This show-stopper—draped in green chiffon and sequined fabric—feels right at home within the light-green walls here in the "For Redheads Only" room, which Max Factor had specially designed for Lucille Ball to complement her fiery red hair.

▲ **Lucy's colors** The ginger and green ornaments shown here reinforce the tree themes: movie glamour and color. The different shapes hint at a showgirl's sexy curves.

▶ **Reflective beauty** A tube of lipstick and a hand mirror are two common elements in a star's makeup case, and Lucy was known for her bright red lipstick. A featured ornament gets its close-up.

JUDY GARLAND

The Girl from Oz

SO MUCH HAS BEEN WRITTEN about Judy Garland that she has become a part of our national consciousness. Her face looks out at us from CDs, birthday cards, book covers, calendars—and even Christmas ornaments—as well as from her many films and television appearances.

Judy Garland doesn't really need another *Wizard of Oz* tribute to be remembered. Yet as I designed her tree, I realized that this was unavoidable. No matter what Judy did throughout her career, she was always "returned to Oz" by her public. So I made ruby red the predominant color and focused on the Ruby Slippers, Dorothy's primary mode of transportation through the land of Oz.

I believe that Judy always felt trapped by the image of Dorothy, the tragic little girl looking for happiness over the rainbow. In truth, the people who were close to Judy knew her to be a brilliant performer with a wicked sense of humor who was passionate about life and full of love for her family. I chose to depict the grown-up Judy on a concert stage, mike in hand, ready to sing—with that yellow brick road never too far away.

◀ The Ruby Slippers In this case, although it's certainly not the largest piece here, this ornament is the main statement piece. The entire tree is designed around them, from the star on top to the red-sequined tree skirt.

▼ The Rainbow The multicolored ball introduces another element from *The Wizard of Oz*, the fabled rainbow that Dorothy sang about. How ironic that the song for which she is best remembered was initially cut from the movie!

◀ Follow the Yellow Brick Road Yellow satin represents the Yellow Brick Road, and on that road are an assortment of press photos, newspaper clippings, memorabilia, and *Wizard of Oz* ornaments—all leading Judy back to her beginning: a little girl from a theatrical family, literally born in a trunk.

BETTE DAVIS & KATHARINE HEPBURN

Hollywood Royalty

"TWO QUEENS, ONE THRONE." This could have been the headline on any given day during the Golden Age of Hollywood. Epic battles were waged between actresses who sought to become "Queen of the Lot," and these wars were wickedly reported by the press.

Bette Davis and Katharine Hepburn each held this title during their careers, but they were queens in two separate kingdoms: Bette at Warner Brothers and Kate at MGM. This presented me with an intriguing idea. I did some research and, according to most historical references, Elizabeth Tudor, Queen of England, and her archrival for the throne, Mary Stuart, Queen of Scotland—although cousins—never met.

What if I brought these two Hollywood queens together to portray the two equally famous historical queens? Bette played Elizabeth twice in her career, and Kate played Mary, but never in the same picture. In fact, Bette and Kate never worked together onstage or onscreen. Since anything is possible in Hollywood, we can finally say that we have brought Bette and Kate together at last in the same "picture."

▼ **Mary's adornments** To recreate Mary's tightly curled hairstyle, textured copper-net ribbon was cut into strips, rolled into curls, and glued to the mannequin's head. A fabric headdress and pearl crown complete the illusion.

▲ **Elizabeth's ornamentals** Prominently featured are fabric ornaments—pearled and bejeweled—to mimic the famous red wigs Elizabeth wore throughout her reign.

◀ **Rivals** The two queens face off on a stairway to signify Mary Stuart's quest to ascend to the throne, which was firmly occupied by Elizabeth Tudor (at the top).

RITA HAYWORTH
—— Put the Blame on Mame ——

THE DEFINING MOMENT I chose for the Rita Hayworth tree was actually near the end of the carnival scene in the 1946 film *Gilda.* Surrounded by an audience of partygoers, Rita's character Gilda, having run out of options for escape, chose defiance as her revenge. Slinking across the screen in a black satin gown, she arrogantly tossed back her auburn hair and peeled off her gloves to the musical strains of "Put the Blame on Mame," and in that moment, Rita Hayworth went from young Hollywood starlet to superstar.

Although the film is in black-and-white, while watching it, I could nevertheless imagine all of the colors that surrounded Gilda, from the blues and purples of the nightclub to the greens and yellows of the decorations. So I surrounded her here in jewel-toned ornamentation.

By keeping the area around the tree in shadow, I created an intimate setting, which represented the darkened supper club in which Gilda performed. As an interesting side note, the two oversized faces bathed in hot pink and lilac light, which appear to float behind the tree, are rumored to have appeared in the outdoor carnival scene in the film. I just liked them because they added drama.

▶ **Party girl** The ultimate party girl, Rita Hayworth as Gilda rises from the center of the tree, which represents the swirl of the carnival surrounding her as she performs. Black satin cuts through the tree and pools on the floor to create a slinky, ruffled tree skirt. Theatrical lighting transforms the satin into vivid shades of red, purple, and blue.

◀ **Musical accompaniment** When Gilda sings "Put the Blame on Mame" for the first time, she is playing the guitar. The way music enhances a movie, the guitar featured here serves to embellish the tree design.

▶ **Mexican hat dance** Sequined felt sombreros add party spirit to the tree. Reputedly, the margarita cocktail was named for Rita when she danced under her real name—Margarita—in a Tijuana club.

DID YOU EVER WONDER what it would be like to go through Mae West's attic? Think about the treasures that you would find there—from what I hear, she never threw anything away!

I got such a chance when the Hollywood History Museum was loaned a large portion of her private collection for a special exhibit. What fun I had . . . so much to play with, so many design choices.

For Mae's tree, I chose to re-create the famous black-and-white dress (seen in the rear of the photograph) that she wore in her final movie, the 1977 film *Sextette*—sequined, furred, and feathered. I added purple and red ornaments to complement several other Mae gowns in the exhibit, which surround the decorated tree. These gowns were featured in her films and stage shows, and they really showed off not only her figure but also her zest for life and her colorful persona.

Mae was very fond of jewelry—she loved to sparkle—so I included many pieces from her own collection and added some diamond-shaped ornaments as well. It was eerie—after the feathered-headdress treetop was added, the tree actually felt and looked like Mae to me. I could almost hear her imploring me to come up sometime and see her.

▲ **This girl's best friend** Whether wearing diamonds or rhinestones, Mae was a walking jewelry store. These rhinestone pieces were some of her favorites.

▶ **Diamond Lil** Her hard-as-diamonds exterior hid her heart of gold from the movie-going public. This oversized "diamond" is a

▶ **Fabric, feathers, and fur** These three elements are the statement pieces in Mae's tree. Combined, they create a wardrobe to dress her from. Sparkling, glittery ornaments stand in for jewelry and become accessories.

GLORIA SWANSON

—— I'm the Greatest Star ——

WHEN GLORIA SWANSON'S character, Norma Desmond, declared "We didn't need dialogue, we had faces then!" in the 1950 film classic *Sunset Boulevard*, she spoke for all the forgotten souls left behind in the wake created by the onset of talking pictures. However, Gloria was not one of them. Her exotic beauty captivated movie audiences for six decades, and eventually she became the sole survivor of an era the world will never see again.

I wanted her tree to reflect a time of excess, when gold, leopard skins, and peacock feathers decorated both fashion and furniture; when silent screen stars drank free-flowing champagne under enormous crystal chandeliers while orchestras played. In other words, I wanted this tree to have a feeling of grand decadence that would represent both Gloria and Norma.

As the dominant color, black provides the foundation for a path into the black-and-white world of Norma Desmond, where beautiful people walked along Sunset Boulevard watched by the audience—to whom Norma Desmond dedicated her final close-up: "those wonderful people out there in the dark."

Wardrobe This flapper-style dress in a leopard print, attached to its ornament hanger and nestled in gold satin, stands for the styish young Hollywood starlet that Norma Desmond once was.

Costars Custom-made fabric-covered balls provide both color and texture. Black is the main through-line, or unifying, color; the leopard print adds dimension and repeats the main pattern. Pearls add luxury.

Ready for my close-up This tree's over-the-top elegance makes it the star of the show. The movie camera and other props play supporting roles without diverting the eye from the main focus.

CHER

——— Just Plain Goddess ———

WHAT MUST IT BE LIKE TO BE CHER? I must confess that Cher is an enigma to me. For as long as I've lived, there has always been Cher. She has conquered the fields of television, music, and film. My love affair with her began when I first saw her on *The Sonny and Cher Show* all those years ago.

I was with her through the Disco Era (as a fan) and was fortunate enough to meet her when I was a lowly intern for *Saturday Night Live* at NBC Studios in New York City when she was hosting the show. My love for her deepened when she "allowed" me to fetch her a bottle of water. Ahhh, the memories!

When designing her tree, I approached it through the eyes of a lifelong fan, someone willing and in fact eager to stand off to the side, lucky enough to be backstage at one of her concerts, watching the Goddess perform.

Cher's tree is topped with beads and a tangle of brunette curls. I covered her tree in sequined fabric, feathers, satin, baubles, and large colorful lights, attempting to emulate the outrageous costumes she's worn throughout her career. I hope I have done her justice.

▼ Designer medallion Cher is known for wearing expensive designer couture. This piece has a beautiful, elegant, upscale design. The color complements the tree and adds an element of sophistication.

▲ Feathered ball Cher has worn many shockingly wild feathered headdresses (by designer Bob Mackie). This inspired me to add feathery fun and use these kicky plumed balls. What better way to say "Cher"?

◄ Stage show Center stage at the Alex Theatre, the tree faces the audience. Seen here is the back of the "costume," outrageous as it is. Yet it never overpowers Cher herself.

BOB'S CELEBRITY ORNAMENTS

My collection of signed ornaments started as a fluke. I was working for Kathy Hilton at her store in West Hollywood. One day Audrey Meadows walked in, and since I was a big fan, I asked for an autograph. Typically, I had nothing for her to sign, so she graciously suggested an ornament—and the rest is history!

1. Patrick Duffy **2.** Ed Begly, Jr. **3.** Gloria Allred **4.** Mariska Hargitay **5.** Maureen McCormick **6.** John Tesh / Connie Sellecca **7.** Lorna Luft **8.** Leslie Nielsen **9.** JM J. Bullock **10.** Stefanie Powers **11.** Suzanne Pleshette **12.** Zubin Mehta **13.** Cheryl Tiegs **14.** Jaclyn Smith **15.** Erik Estrada **16.** Jennifer Tilly **17.** Mary Hart **18.** Jo Anne Worley **19.** Richard Simmons **20.** Donny Osmond **21.** Constance Towers **22.** Ashford & Simpson **23.** Joanna Kern **24.** Marion Ross **25.** Joan Van Ark **26.** Delta Burke **27.** Carol Channing **28.** Daryl Hannah **29.** Audrey Meadows **30.** Kate Jackson **31.** David Cassidy **32.** Bernadette Peters **33.** Rosie O'Donnell **34.** Helen Reddy **35.** Mary Frann **36.** Nancy Reagan **37.** Dolores Hope **38.** Bob Hope **39.** Shirley MacLaine **40.** Priscilla Presley **41.** Ann Miller **42.** Angela Lansbury **43.** Jack Lemmon **44.** Lynn Redgrave **45.** Joan Collins **46.** Ed Asner **47.** Jane Seymour **48.** Vicki Lawrence **49.** Robert Stack **50.** Cyd Charisse **51.** Shelley Winters **52.** Lauren Bacall **53.** Candice Bergen **54.** Estelle Getty **55.** Sally Kellerman **56.** Valerie Harper **57.** Nell Carter **58.** Leslie Uggams **59.** Brenda Russell **60.** Garry Marshall **61.** Leeza Gibbons **62.** Dick Clark **63.** Phyllis Diller

3

TREE STYLING & TRIMMINGS

*P*utting a tree together is like making a movie. The tree must be "scripted" as well as cast. In other words, choose a theme, then select your ornamental "actors." Decorations are like stars, costars and extras. You, as the designer, get to direct your own movie. The following pages will guide you on where to start, what is available, and how to end up with the perfectly produced feature.

TREE LOCATION

Finding the right spot to set up your Christmas tree seems like an easy thing to do. Most of us simply choose a spot in the living room and put the tree there. But the place you would like the tree to go is not always the best place for your tree.

SITING YOUR TREE

First, decide what your tree is going to be used for: Family and package opening on Christmas Day? Will you even be home on Christmas?

▲ **Family gatherings** This long hall leads to a tree in the drawing room, where family can gather to celebrate.

Will the tree be a centerpiece for parties? Do you want to make it a canvas to show off your children's art or collectibles? Answering these questions will help you decide on the best location.

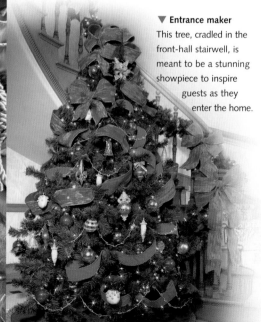

▼ **Entrance maker**
This tree, cradled in the front-hall stairwell, is meant to be a stunning showpiece to inspire guests as they enter the home.

Your tree may look beautiful in the front hall, but will it be comfortable to sit around it on a cold floor on Christmas morning? Or should you consider placing it in a room where your friends and family will be cozier?

Consider decorating more than one tree. One can be for show: to get your guests into the holiday spirit the minute they walk in the door. The other can be warm and inviting, and put in a place where you can spend quality time with your guests.

POWER, HEAT & LIGHT

There should be an electrical outlet in the location that you're considering. You can use extension cords, but the farther lights are from the outlet, the more likely they are to burn out. Also, shorter cords eliminate the possibility of someone tripping.

Also consider environmental factors. Live trees should be kept away from "hot spots." If you place a live tree near a working fireplace, in direct sunlight, or near heating vents, the tree will dry out quickly and could become a fire hazard. While sunlight may not adversely affect your artificial tree, it can fade all of your decorations: fabric, ribbon, ornaments, dolls, and tree skirts can all be irreparably damaged.

SPACE

Next, how much space can you allow for your tree? Measure a tree's width and height before buying it. It helps to move furniture around before dragging

▲ **Alcove spaces** Placing your tree in a bay window or alcove creates a tableau, out of the flow of foot traffic.

the tree into the room. Make sure the tree won't impede the natural flow of foot traffic or interfere with safe exiting in case of an emergency.

PET SAFETY

Pet-proofing is not foolproof. However, there are a few things you can do to protect both your tree and your pet. Be sure to anchor your tree so that if it gets bumped (or your cat climbs up the branches), it won't come crashing down. And to limit access to the tree, either place it on a table if possible or build a barrier of boxes or even decorative fencing around it.

▲ **Elevated beauty** If you own pets, it may be safer to place a small tree on a table or other piece of furniture.

ARTIFICIAL VS LIVE TREES

Christmas trees represent a gathering place for family and friends, an emotional connection to the past, and an expression of creativity. Therefore, tree selection can be very personal, but there are practical factors to consider before you decide, such as the ones in the box below.

FACTORS	ARTIFICIAL TREES	LIVE TREES
PRICE	Cost is higher the first year—but since artificial trees are reusable, after the initial investment, you'll have a tree you can use for many years.	Prices vary depending on local availability, height, and style of tree. Generally, live trees are less expensive than artificial ones.
DISPLAY SPACE	They come in a wide variety of shapes and sizes—from slim-line to full-figured and from tabletop to mall-sized monsters—and are more versatile spacewise.	Many live trees are quite bushy. If space is limited, consider placing a shorter tree on a stable tree-riser, like a coffee table, side table, large wooden crate, or toy chest.
STORAGE SPACE	Storage is an issue if you buy an artificial tree. Ideally, the tree should be stored vertically, in its original package. Old sheets and tree-storage bags also work. Make sure you have clearance to get your tree to the storage space, which must be dry (and should be cool). Artificial trees may mildew in damp environments.	If you don't have room to store a tree, live is the way to go. Use it and lose it. Or, for the environmentally concerned, buy a potted tree and plant it outside if weather conditions permit.
STYLES	Artificial trees are symmetrical, and they can be shaped several ways to give different looks with just one tree. They come in a wide range of colors, including realistic-looking greens, retro silvers, and alternative pink, and "umbrella" hinges make assembly a snap. Sizes, shapes, and branch materials vary, so look around before making a purchase.	Pines, firs, and spruces are the most common trees used for decorating. Live trees are not perfect or symmetrical, so expect to search through unevenly spaced and missing branches, bent trunks, and imperfect tops. Flocking with artificial snow is available in many areas.
LIGHTS & DECORATIONS	Artificial trees need more lights to properly show off your decorations because of the density of branches. You can permanently light the tree, but it will take longer and you'll need more lights than for a live tree. However, many trees now come prelit. Set it up, plug it in, and decorate!	Live trees need fewer lights because of the shape and more spacious positioning of their branches. They are quicker to light and easy to unlight. They also need fewer decorations since they are bushier.
MAINTENANCE & FIRE SAFETY	Make sure to buy a flame-retardant tree: you can put it up whenever you want and wherever you want (as long as it's near an electrical outlet). Artificial trees will never dry out and become fire hazards, so you can put them up early and keep them up as late as you want. Valentine's Day and Easter trees, anyone?	The tree base should be freshly cut, so that your tree can "drink" water properly. Tree stands usually hold at least a gallon of water. Keep the tree watered throughout the holidays, and refill as needed. To keep your tree from drying out and becoming a fire hazard, keep it away from heat sources like fireplaces, heating vents, and direct sunlight, and keep the temperature down.
ACCIDENTS	Children and pets are attracted to both artificial and live trees. Minimize risks by elevating your tree, and/or building a barrier with packages, miniature villages, or fencing. Trees can be anchored to the wall with fishing line to prevent accidents.	Same as artificial trees, see left.
ALLERGIES	Dust accumulation over the years can cause allergic reactions. Dust your tree with a feather duster before storing, or use artificial-tree cleaning products to help prevent allergies.	Live trees can cause or exacerbate allergies, so if you or a family member suffers from hay fever, asthma, or any other respiratory ailment, an artificial tree is the better option.
INSECTS	Insects—and especially spiders—like to hide in stored artificial trees. Proper airtight storage and an annual dusting can prevent spider infestation.	Insects may be hiding in your tree. Shake the tree well before bringing it into your home.

ARTIFICIAL TREE SELECTION

In the artificial tree, the beauty of nature has been recreated with a few "plusses." The branches are evenly spaced, giving you a tree that can be decorated symmetrically. Trunks come unbent, and treetops are perfectly vertical so whatever you place on top stands straight. Artificial trees come in one or several pieces (depending on size); lit or unlit; in traditional or alternative shapes; and in a multitude of colors, widths, and heights. They are even available fully decorated.

When selecting your tree, consider the size of your decorations. Here, the wide spaces between branches are excellent for highlighting your collectibles.

▲ Spiky mountain pine   ▲ Rounded opalescent fir

▲ Light-colored blue spruce

▲ Frosted, with pinecones and berries

► **Full, dense branches**
Most basic-shaped artificial trees have denser branches than live trees.

▲ **Needle types** A wide range of shapes, textures, lengths, and colors is available to the artificial-tree lover: long, short, round, blunt, soft, stiff, with pinecones and berries, frosted, and in every color under the sun.

TRADITIONAL TREES

The custom of decorating fir trees for Christmas dates back to 16th-century Germany. The tradition traveled throughout Europe and eventually became popular in the New World. By the mid-1800s, Bavarian fir forests had dwindled, prompting German entrepreneurs to produce the first artificial Christmas trees.

The first faux trees were crafted of metal wires and covered with the decorative feathers of large birds like geese, ostriches, swans, and turkeys, usually dyed green. Feather trees

remained in vogue for many years, but they were limited in their ability to hold large or heavy decorations.

In the 1930s, the Addis Brush Company in the United States crafted the first artificial tree out of the same animal bristles they used to make toilet brushes (but dyed green), and "bottlebrush" trees hit the market. These trees were larger and sturdier than feather trees, and they could support heavier ornaments. Today, you can find artificial trees that are incredible reproductions of live trees, in a variety of styles almost as limitless as in nature.

◄ **Tiered construction** This novelty tree comes with widely separated branches that provide you with layers or tiers. It is a great showcase tree for train tracks, lit villages, or other collectibles.

TREE WIDTH & HEIGHT

If you're having space issues, there are a number of ways in which to compensate. One way to create the illusion of a much larger tree—and save money—is to place a small or medium-sized tree on a low, sturdy table. Elevating the tree also leaves more room for wrapped presents, train sets, Christmas villages, and nativity scenes. Another possibility is to try a trio-grouping with narrow slim-line or pencil trees bunched closely together: either use three different-sized trees, or use three of the same size, but placed at different height levels to create a natural, staggered look.

HEIGHT COUNTS

The taller an artificial tree is, the more expensive it is, so here are two money-saving tips for added height: tree stands may add an inch or two; and a tall treetop decoration can extend a tree's height by a foot or more.

◄ **Thick, bushy branches** This medium-sized tree is accented with opalescent needles, giving it a shimmery quality.

▲ **Pencil trees** With their narrow construction and light, wispy, downswept branches, these trees provide petite splashes of greenery and need minimal decoration.

TIME & SPACE SAVERS

For people with extremely limited time and/or tight space, enterprising inventors have created roll-up and coiling trees—usually predecorated—that can literally be installed in seconds. Wall half-trees are available and especially helpful in dorm rooms, small apartments, and offices. And you can even buy a tree lit with both clear and several colors of lights. Plug in this gimmicky tree and choose one of several light colors in one of several patterns. You can change the light colors of your tree as easily as unplugging one stack of plugs and plugging in another. Then, with a remote control, change the light pattern and colors as often as you like.

◄ **Roll it away** This clever prelit, predecorated wall half-tree rolls up into about one cubic foot. It's perfect for small rooms and offices.

▶ **Decorated spiral** Another entry in the "instant decoration" category is this spiraling tree. The center support pole is removable. After the season, the tree flattens into a box the size of a jumbo pizza.

▶ **Five-color light changer** This tree offers the versatility of lights in red, green, blue, gold, and clear, or any combination of lights you might like—as well as several pattern options.

Clear miniature light bulb

Multicolored miniature light bulb

C-7 light cover

NONTRADITIONAL TREES

The silver and white trees popular in the 1950s and '60s have had several comebacks over the years. Now, these "retro" trees are made with newer, safer materials, and you can make quite a fashion statement by choosing from a wide range of colors, including black, gold, red, pastels—even custom-blends of several colors. The trees come in sizes ranging from miniature tabletop to full-sized. If you choose to light your medium-to-large fashion-color tree, buy white cord light sets for lighter-colored trees, and green for darker tones; gold cords, for gold trees, are available as well. For miniature trees featured as lit-tabletop decorations, use battery-run lights.

If you're looking for something nontraditional, consider trees made of poinsettias, berries, or metal wire, or even alternative trees such as light-rope palm trees or upside-down trees. Newer fiber-optic trees don't provide much light, but they look quite dramatic in a dark room. Every year, innovative trees appear on the market with some new twist on lighting or music—like a tree attached to a box that makes your lights "dance" to music. So keep your options open—there are trees out there for everyone.

▲ **Fashion colors** These colorful trees in pink, silver, black, white, and gold are a small sampling of the array of colors available for trees in today's marketplace.

◀ **Color wheel** The revolving, tinted color wheel—a hold-out from the 1960s—is meant to be shined on a silver tree to create changing color effects.

▲ **Fiber-optic flair** To avoid blocking the tips of fiber-optic light, don't use large bows or wide ribbon. The tree center is unlit, so keep ornaments near branch tips.

▲ **Fiber-optic poinsettia** For indoor use only, this novelty tree makes a good decoration for a hall entryway. No ornaments or lights are needed, so just plug it in and fluff it.

▲ **Decorative wire** This display piece can hold several of your favorite ornaments, and it makes a good unlit tabletop decoration.

▲ **Lit palms** Looking for the most unusual display piece for the holidays? These prelit tropical trees fit the bill.

LIVE TREE SELECTION

There are many types of live trees available to use for Christmas. Although live trees are imperfect and often have bent trunks, missing branches, or asymmetrical tops, none of this matters to the live-tree purist. Problems can be hidden with creative decorating, like strategic placement of statement pieces or bows. Sometimes a lopsided tree can be doctored: if branches are missing, you can bore holes into the trunk and replace them. (This has even been done on New York's Rockefeller Center tree.)

TREE CHOICES

Live-tree choice will be influenced by availability in your area. The chart below provides some insight into the pros and cons of each tree type. Knowledge of needle retention is especially key. Trees that drop needles quickly should be bought just two weeks before Christmas to stay fresh indoors. Some trees, like the blue spruce, are so beautiful and ornamental that they are becoming popular as potted "living" Christmas trees that can be planted outside after the holiday season. Prices for live trees depend on the number of years it takes a tree to mature, growing conditions, and demand for each particular tree. However, most people still choose a tree simply based on its appearance.

TREE	COLORADO BLUE SPRUCE	NORWAY SPRUCE	NOBLE FIR	DOUGLAS FIR	SCOTCH PINE	EASTERN WHITE PINE	AUSTRIAN PINE
NEEDLE COLOR	Bluish gray-green	Medium green	Gray-green to bright blue-gray	Dark green	Bright to blue to dark green	Blue-green to silver-green	Dark green
NEEDLE TYPE	Short, stiff	Short (on longer branches), soft	Short and twisted upward, soft	Very short, soft	Short to long depending on cultivar, stiff	Long, soft	Very long, stiff but flexible
AREA	Western to northwestern US	Northeastern US, southeastern Canada, Europe	Pacific west coast; Danish noble firs available in Europe	Western Canada to California; exported to Hawaii, Guam & Asian markets	Northeastern, central & Pacific US; Canada, Europe & Asia	Most of continental US, excluding Gulf & West Coasts	Northeastern, central US; southern Canada, south & central Europe
NEEDLE RETENTION	2 to 3 weeks	1 to 2 weeks	6 weeks to 3 months	6 weeks to 3 months	4 to 6 weeks	4 to 5 weeks	4 to 5 weeks

TREE SETUP

Before setting up your tree, protect yourself—wear long sleeves and gloves to prevent cuts, and use something soft to kneel on (especially for artificial-tree setup, which takes a bit of time) to save you from aches and pains later. Both artificial and live trees shed needles, so after setup, vacuum or sweep before decorating to prevent the static-prone needles from adhering to everything in sight.

POTTED LIVE TREES

When purchasing a live, potted tree for Christmas, ask the nursery or tree lot how to care for the tree both during and after the holidays. Each species requires unique care. If you live in a cold climate, you may not be able to replant it outdoors until spring thaw. Be prepared to care for your potted tree indoors until then.

TREE STANDS

Tree stands weren't needed for the very first Christmas trees in Germany, during the Middle Ages, because people cut off the treetops and nailed the trees to the ceiling upside-down. When trees were finally set upright, a simple "X" of two boards was nailed to the tree bottom to serve as a stand. Next, trees were potted in baskets, pots, or urns and steadied with dirt and rocks. The first commercial stands appeared in the late 1800s with the advent of larger trees. Cast iron was popular for its weight and for how well it supported trees. Later designs, like the three-legged tripod, allowed for lightweight plastic construction.

ARTIFICIAL TREE STANDS

▲ Metal cross "X" stand

▲ Round plastic with on/off switch

LIVE TREE STANDS

▲ Decorative metal stand

▲ Round tiered plastic

Artificial tree setup

After finding the perfect spot for your artificial tree, make sure to protect your floor. Whether you have wood, tile, or another type of floor, and especially if you have carpeting, prevent damage by following a few easy steps. Move furniture out of the way, if necessary, before bringing your tree in. Place a piece of cardboard on the floor where the tree stand will go, to help you move the tree before and after decorating. It makes vacuuming, sweeping, or dusting easier because you can pull the tree around by the cardboard. Before assembly, lay out the pieces of your tree. The number of pieces will vary, depending on the tree size and style. Most new trees have umbrella- or hinge-assembly and come in three pieces. Follow the manufacturer's instructions provided.

BRANCHES

Bungeeing the branches while assembling your tree, and letting them down row by row, makes shaping quick and safe by preventing scratches.

PRELIT TREES

If your artificial tree is prelit, continue on to steps 4–6 on the next page to finish setting up your tree. If you'll be attaching lighting to your artificial tree, you should light each branch immediately after you shape it—continue from here on to page 140–41, and follow the directions for Lighting an Artificial Tree.

1 Assemble the tree stand according to directions and set on the center of the cardboard. Place the bottom of the tree into the stand. Check to make sure the stand doesn't wobble; adjust if needed.

2 Wrap up all branches with bungee cords, except for the bottom row. Keep in mind that you don't have to shape the tree perfectly—you want it to look as natural as possible.

3 Starting at the trunk, grab the first two "greens" and pull them in opposing directions at an angle. Move out to the next two; angle perpendicularly to the first set. Continue along the branch, alternating angles. Pull the end green out and angle it slightly up.

LIVE TREE SETUP

It is as important to protect your floor when installing a live tree as when installing an artificial one—maybe even more so. First, move furniture and place cardboard down on the floor where the tree will go. Take the extra step of placing plastic sheeting or a tree bag on top of the cardboard to prevent water damage to your floor.

If you buy your tree at a lot, you can ask the salesperson to secure a wood stand to the base of the tree. Or, if your tree does not come with an attached

DROOPY BRANCH TIP

To raise up low-hanging branches on your live tree, and to make more room for trains, villages, or presents, try attaching a piece of floral wire to the middle of the low-hanging branch. Pull the branch just a little higher than you want it, and then attach the other end of the wire to a higher branch.

stand, then assemble your own tree stand first and place it at the center of the plastic-covered cardboard.

Shake your tree to get rid of loose needles and insects, and bring it inside. Water the tree immediately to extend its life. Make adjustments if your tree is not standing perfectly straight.

Since live tree branches will droop within a day or two of setup and can cover gifts or other under-tree items, you may want to prune back any that are too low, or tie them up with floral wire (see *Droopy Branch Tip*, left). It also helps to cut away a branch or two near the base to allow room to water your tree.

PET SAFETY

Do not permit your pets to dig in the potting soil in your Christmas tree stand; the soil and water may contain toxins that will irritate their digestive systems.

▲ Monofilament or fishing line

▲ Eye hooks

Anchor your tree so that it cannot be pulled over by a child or pet. Fishing line and eye hooks are a great way to insure safety for all. If your tree is near curtain rods or sturdy poles or pillars, you can attach fishing line to one, then run it to the top third of your tree and back to another attachment point. If these aren't available, place an eye hook or a nail in the wall. Attach a piece of fishing line to the eye hook or nail, then run the line to the top third of the tree and then to another eye hook or nail at a 90-degree angle from the first one.

Shape the treetop before putting it in place to give it a more natural look.

Pull outer branches out and up if they got bent during setup.

4 Move on to the next branch, and continue around the whole row until complete. Remove the bungee cord and let down the next row above. Continue shaping until you finish this part of the tree. Insert the next tree part and repeat from step 3.

5 The treetop requires slightly different shaping. Before placing it on the tree, grab each green, starting at the trunk, and pull it up and out. Then put your treetop in place and blend the branches between the middle tree section and the treetop.

6 The finished tree. Remember: the more time you spend fluffing the branches, the easier the tree will be to light and decorate, and the better it will look.

LIGHTING

Until the late 19th century, Christmas trees were lit with candles. Three years after Thomas Edison invented the electric light bulb in 1879, an associate of his, Edward Johnson, put the first electric lights on a Christmas tree—paving the way for the evolution of Christmas lights into the spectacular array of styles now available on the market.

LIGHTING AN ARTIFICIAL TREE

The tree lighting shown here will help you turn an unlit tree into a permanently lit tree that doesn't have to be relit every year. Although you can buy a prelit tree, you may choose to light your own because you already own a nice artificial tree, or because you'd like to custom design the lights. Make sure you have enough bulbs on hand to light the tree and to allow for replacement bulbs and strings in the future. Do not mix bulbs. Voltages and bulb housings may vary among manufacturers.

While sets of 100 bulbs are okay for live trees, use sets of 50 for permanently lighting an artificial tree. 100s are really two sets of 50 spliced together, and frequent handling of the cords may cause half the set to burn out. Look for lights with generous spacing between bulbs to give your lighting a cleaner look with less cord-crossover.

▶ Do not permanently wire C-7 or C-9 bulbs to an artificial tree; they are fragile and don't store well. Remove them at the end of the season.

Lighting method

Artificial-tree lighting varies from live-tree lighting. You must light each section of the tree separately if you want to store the tree in pieces. The artificial tree will be lit row by row, starting at the bottom. Before lighting, assemble and bungee your tree as shown in steps 1–3 in Artificial Tree Setup on page 138. Do not light it in vertical thirds, as demonstrated on the live tree, on page 142.

CORD COLORS

White cord lights were used here for demonstration purposes only to make it easier for you to follow the steps provided. Use green cords for green and any other dark-colored trees, white cords for white and pastel trees, and gold cords for gold trees.

1 Plug in your lights. Make two loops with the cord spaced between the lights closest to the plug end.

2 Insert one loop into the other and pull that loop through tightly to make a noose.

3 Start near the tree trunk on the bottom row. Slip the open loop over an inner green, slide it down, and pull tight.

6 Wrap lights around the next green near its tip, then wrap back to the branch. For moderate lighting, wrap every third green; for showcase lighting, wrap every green (see top of page 141).

7 Continue working back to the trunk. As you go, cross the cord over and around the branch occasionally to secure it. When you near the trunk, wrap the cord around the second-to-last green.

8 Move on to the next branch and keep adding lights. When you finish one row, move on to the next, remove the bungee cord, and continue lighting until you reach the end of each tree section.

Lighting intensity styles

Determine how brightly you want your tree to be lit. Trees in dark display areas need fewer lights. Denser trees need more lights to help show off your ornaments.

▲ **Fully lit branch with subtle lighting** This is an inexpensive option that works well for a sparse style. Simply stretch the cord back to the center after you complete step 5, below; then secure, and move on to the next branch.

▲ **Fully lit branch with moderate lighting** Here, every third green is wrapped. This style looks good on trees that have longer needles and an average number of branches. It also provides more light to show off ornaments if your tree is near a window or in a brightly lit area.

▲ **Fully lit branch with full showcase lighting** For the most intense, dramatic lighting, light every green. This is the most expensive and labor-intensive option, but it's well worth it: every one of your ornaments will sparkle and shine!

LIGHT AMOUNTS

For lighting a standard 7-foot tree, you need approximately 15 sets of 50s for subtle lighting; 25 sets of 50s for moderate lighting; and up to 60 sets of 50s for full, dramatic showcase lighting.

LIGHTS THAT LAST

You should use no more than 300 lights in a row before starting back at the power strip (or wall plug); otherwise, they are likely to short out. Power strips are recommended, due to the number of lights that will be in use.

After lighting the tree, blend the branches wherever new tree sections start.

4 Working on the branch where you have made the first loop, pull the lights from the center of the tree all of the way out toward the tip of the branch.

5 Wrap the light string around the outermost green twice. If you want subtle lighting, skip steps 6–8 and refer instead to the far left caption above; then proceed to step 9.

9 To light the treetop, begin a new light set. Start at the bottom, and wrap occasional greens, following the wrapping technique in steps 1–4. Since the treetop is denser than the body of the tree, you only need to light every third or fourth green.

10 Moderate lighting such as this is adequate for most tree styles. This tree is lit with miniature, multicolored bulbs—you can also try all clear, all one color, or a combination of any or all of these.

LIGHTING A LIVE TREE

Because you cannot permanently light live trees, they offer you the opportunity to play with color design like an artist with a blank canvas. The tree doesn't have to be lit with only clear, multicolor, or single-color lights. Try mixing several single-color light sets in colors that complement your decorations. Or you can create irregular blocks of color by stringing three cords of one color together and placing them on one section of the tree, then go on to plug in three more sets of another color and continue lighting the next tree section.

Many people walk around and around a live tree to light it, randomly wrapping the branches to keep the lights secure. The problem with this technique is that as the tree dries, the branches snag your cords and make unlighting the tree difficult at the end of the holidays. It is best not to wrap live branches at all; laying light sets on the branches offers better illumination for your special ornaments and makes light-set removal quick and easy.

The technique we use calls for lighting your tree in thirds: simply layer the lights on the tops of branches with minimal anchoring and light only one-third of the tree at a time. When it comes time to remove the lights after Christmas, you can stand in one place, pull on each light string, and strip the tree without any cord tangling. Of course, this only applies to miniature light sets. Clipped-on C-7s and C-9s should be carefully removed bulb by bulb.

▶ **Multicolor magic** A live tree lit with C-9s provides subtle light.

Lighting made easy

The lighting technique shown here is for trees with relatively flat branches. For bushier trees like the Douglas fir, apply the same principles—but since there is no natural branch spacing, weave lights in and out starting at the bottom row, then move up about 1 foot and repeat. This technique assures virtually no visible light cords.

SIMPLE REMOVAL

When you lay lights on branches instead of wrapping them, light removal at the end of the season is quick, easy, and less messy!

CORD COLORS

Use green cords—white-cord lights were used for demonstration purposes only to make it easier to follow the steps provided.

1 Plug your lights into a power strip. Starting near the trunk of the tree, at the bottom, place lights on a branch nearest the trunk and stretch them out toward that branch's tip.

2 Using a "ribbon-candy" pattern, begin to cover the branch with lights. Once the branch is uniformly covered, pull the light set back toward the tree trunk.

3 Lightly secure the lights to an inner green by separating the light cords and poking about an inch of green through the hole. This will prevent the lights from slipping.

4 Move on to the next branch and repeat this process on the third of the tree facing you. Move up from branch row to branch row as needed until you reach the top.

TROUBLESHOOTING: IF SOME OR ALL OF THE TREE WON'T LIGHT

ONE-SET QUICK FIX

1. First, check that all light sets are plugged into an outlet or power strip, and that the power strip is turned on. Also check light-set plugs; if one has burned out, replace the whole string.

2. If your light sets have fuses, check that they are not burned. If you find a blackened, burned-out fuse, replace it.

3. Make sure circuit breakers were not tripped. If using multiple light sets, you may need to divide them between two different outlets, each on a separate breaker, using extension cords. Use a power strip for each outlet, and plug only one extension cord into each strip.

4. Check for missing or burned-out bulbs. At the same time, you should "run the string"—push on every bulb to check for loose ones. There are several types of light sets. Some go out entirely if a bulb burns out. Another type stays lit if a bulb burns out, but goes out if a bulb pops out. The newest sets will stay lit even if one or more bulbs pop out of their sockets, but these sets are only available regionally and are pricier than traditional sets. If a bulb is black, just replace that bulb. Burned-out bulbs should be immediately replaced. Leaving them in causes the entire set to burn out more quickly.

▶ Burned-out bulb

5. If pushing on the bulbs doesn't work, try removing each bulb. There are two wires that must make a connection to the sides of the socket in order for the bulb to light. Make sure that each is straight and long enough to touch the socket. Straighten the wires and place the bulb back in its socket.

6. If a wire is missing or too short to make contact, replace the bulb. However, this approach takes time if you have to replace multiple lights. If, after replacing one bulb, the set still won't light, just replace the whole set.

▶ Bulb with one shorter wire

7. As a last resort, unplug the dead set, remove it (cutting it in a few places speeds up the process), and replace it. Do NOT cut plugged-in or still-functioning cords!

A quick fix for one dead set—especially if your tree is already decorated—is to plug in a new set and simply lay the lights into the "dead area." Place lights carefully, making sure to work them deep into the tree.

For artificial trees that you wish to light permanently, this is only a temporary fix: before you store your tree for the year, remember to remove the temporary light set, then remove the dead set and replace it with working lights.

Never permanently affix new, working light sets over nonworking ones. Layering set upon set causes the greenery to flatten and will leave you with an unbushy branch of light cords. Remember: For easy unlighting, use sets of 50s on artificial trees.

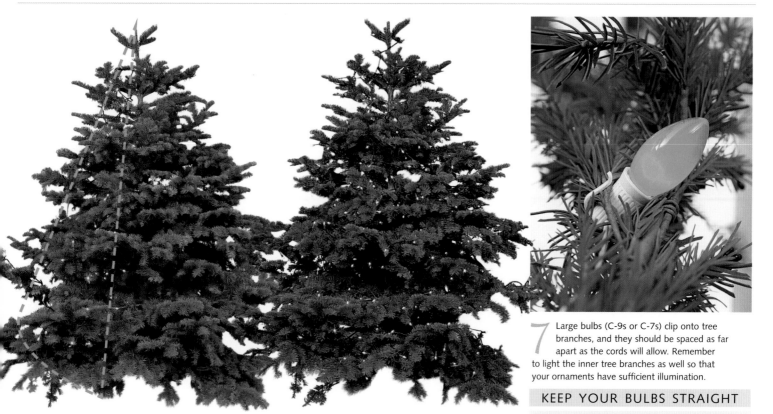

5 After one-third of the tree is lit, as shown above, move onto the next third. Start at the bottom and repeat steps 1–4.

6 When you're done, the tree will be uniformly lit. If you have extra lights left over when you reach the top of the tree, work back toward the bottom.

7 Large bulbs (C-9s or C-7s) clip onto tree branches, and they should be spaced as far apart as the cords will allow. Remember to light the inner tree branches as well so that your ornaments have sufficient illumination.

KEEP YOUR BULBS STRAIGHT

Position C-7s and C-9s to point straight up. If the tree droops in a day or two, readjust them.

LIGHTING STYLES

The sheer variety of lights to choose from is as dazzling as the lights themselves. Here is a description of the different bulb types—from minatures to medium-sized to large novelty bulbs—to help you sort through the maze:

Miniatures, or "mini" lights, are standard incandescent bulbs ranging from 2.5–5 volts.

LED stands for "light emitting diode," and these lights are relatively new to the Christmas arena. They are energy efficient, long-lasting, and they burn cooler.

C-7s and C-9s are large, incandescent lights in the 5–7 volt range, with glass or ceramic bulbs.

Novelty/alternative lights come in a variety of shapes and sizes; this category includes rice lights, which are popular in floral design; fiber optics; bubble lights; and even licensed figures and shapes.

Light-cover attachment

Light covers and caps are decorative accessories that slide directly over mini lights and add color, texture, and style. They come in an endless assortment of shapes, are generally made of plastic and metal, and are easy to install.

1 Slip a miniature light bulb into the bottom of the light cover. Press hard to make sure it is secure.

2 Position the cover so that it won't fall off. If it has a cord, secure the cord to a green.

Pigtail attachment

Pigtails are specialty lights that attach to sets of mini lights. Pigtail plugs fit into most standard miniature light sets. They may light, spin, or both. Bend branches out of the way for spinners so they can rotate freely.

1 Remove the light bulb from its housing, and store it so you can replace it when storing your tree.

2 Plug the pigtail into the empty socket. Wrap excess cord around a branch or green.

LIGHT GALLERY

Note: see pages 187–89 for supplier information

MINI LIGHTS

1 Bouquet of fashion colors from seven strands
2 Bouquet of clear lights on green, white, and gold cords

LED LIGHTS

3 Multicolor LED stars
4 New rounded-tip type

C-7s, C-9s & C-50s

5 Round globe opaque multicolor set of C-50s (these fit into C-7 sockets)
6 Multicolored C-7s on green cord
7 Pink C-7s on white cord

NOVELTY LIGHTING

8 Silicone spiky bulb on decorative lamp base
9 White Father Christmas bulb on decorative lamp base
10 Multicolored berry lights
11 Silver and gold berry lights
12 Multicolor diamond pattern (precapped on mini lights)
13 Specialty preattached aluminum star-shaped reflectors on multicolored C-7s
14 Fiber-optic lights
15 Rice lights
16 Tool set: hammer, screwdriver, pliers, and saw
17 Candle-flame-shaped frosted-glass lights
18 Chili peppers
19 Purple light sphere
20 Red rope lights
21 Red electric-ribbon lights
22 Silicone spiky lights
23 Flicker flames
24 Clear glitter-bubble light
25 Multicolored bubble light
26 Church and Christmas tree bubble lights

LIGHT CAPS & COVERS

27 Multicolored PVC (polyvinyl chloride) bulb caps
28 Clear acrylic 3-D star
29 Fabric Santa-hat light cover
30 Jewel-tone, glittered shatterproof globes
31 Tear-shaped, sculpted glass light covers
32 Clear acrylic church

PIGTAILS

33 Glass candle with miniature mirror
34 Ornament spinner: glittered snowman with hanging strawberry ornament
35 Glittered gold lamp
36 Faux-beaded acrylic golden apple
37 Red lantern-sconce

SNOW

Snow is breathtaking when it blankets the branches of
evergreen trees and glistens in the sun, so it was natural for
tree designers to come up with ways to recreate that dazzling
look indoors. Artificial snow gives your tree a homey feel,
conjuring up images of cool winter mornings in a
mountain lodge. Retro-design trees are particularly suited
to "faux snow" because of the contrast between the stark
snow and the large, colorful lights and ornaments.

FLUFF OR SPRAY?

Artificial spray snow is recommended for live trees only, since
the dried spray snow will clump and rub off your artificial
tree when you take it down. If you want a frosty look on an
artificial tree, buy a preflocked or prefrosted tree. You can
create a unique look by snowing an artificial tree yourself
using cotton and sprinkle snow, following the below
method. (This is not a good technique for live trees, since
their branches droop and the unanchored snow falls off.)
You should light your tree before snowing it, but take
care to keep all types of snow away from light sockets.

Snowing an artificial tree

To create the illusion of snow on an artificial tree, it's best to start with fire-
retardant, soft-cotton batting. You also need artificial bagged snow. There are
several kinds on the market—the most realistic-looking is the fluffy Styrofoam
type. The look is finished off with pastel-tint opalescent glitter. Off-white,
vintage mica snow is best for use with old decorations; white snow makes
aged pieces look dirty. Look for faux snow in your local craft or holiday stores.

▲ **Presnowed artificial tree**
This tree appears lightly
dusted with snow.

MATERIALS NEEDED

▲ Cotton batting

▲ Styrofoam-type artificial snow

▲ Antique "mica" snow

▲ Opalescent snow

1 Tear off a small piece of cotton batting. Place it into the tree on a
branch and smooth it down. Pull the end toward the branch tip.
Shape the snow mound into a natural shape. As with spray snow,
don't cover every branch, every third or fourth one is fine. Otherwise,
the snow will overpower the other decorations.

SNOWING A LIVE TREE

Spray snowing is ideal for live trees. When applying, don't spray every single branch tip or it will look unnatural. When snow falls on trees naturally, it creates random patches; this is the look you are trying to recreate. Practice on a piece of paper first, or better still, outside. Also avoid spraying snow directly onto ornaments, bows, or ribbon, as it will permanently stain.

◀ **Tree-lot flocking** If you don't want to spray your tree yourself, many tree lots will cover them for you right at the lot with a huge flocking machine, giving you a very snowy effect.

▲ **Flocked branches** Flocking comes in many different colors: blue, yellow, green, pink, even black.

SPRAY-SNOW SAFETY

Be careful not to spray directly into light sockets to avoid shorting out your lights. Also keep pets and small children away from flocking; it can be toxic if ingested in large quantities.

▲ **Spray-snow technique** Use a light, sweeping motion to avoid unnatural clumps. Spray branch tips only, and vary the amount of snow you use from branch to branch to make it look like the snow fell naturally.

LIGHT & HEAT

Hair spray is flammable and must be kept away from heat sources like fireplaces, heating vents, and larger Christmas light bulbs. Also, do not use spray glue in place of hair spray—it will yellow the cotton. Take special care to check that light bulbs do not touch the snow.

2 To make cleanup easier, lay plastic on the floor under the tree to catch the excess sprinkled snow. Lightly cover each cotton patch with artificial bagged snow to give it texture.

3 Lightly dust each cotton patch once again, this time with opalescent glitter, which simulates sunlight on new-fallen snow. Cover the entire patch, but don't overdo it.

4 Lightly mist each snowy patch with hair spray to set it. Be careful not to aim the spray directly into light sockets. Don't saturate the cotton—a light spray is sufficient. The finished tree is now ready to decorate.

STATEMENT PIECES

A STATEMENT PIECE is anything you choose to feature in or near your tree as a focal point or specialty decoration. Some statement pieces can stand alone as tabletop decorations, but may also work well in trees, wreaths, or garlands. You can have a grouping of related pieces, like a collection of carnival masks—just make sure that your statement pieces are bright, colorful, or eye-catching. Leave enough space around each piece so it won't be hidden behind branches, ornaments, or trimmings.

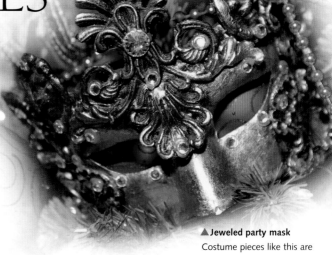

▲ **Jeweled party mask**
Costume pieces like this are stylish and create a fun mood.

ENDLESS VARIETY

Statement pieces can be the jumping-off point for "theming" your tree. For example, on a kids' tree, showcase large stuffed animals surrounded by smaller action figures; a pet tree might feature ornaments shaped like your favorite breed, with dog bones or cat toys as supporting elements. If you're an art lover, create an art-gallery tree with family drawings and photographs, framed or mounted on foamboard. Gardeners can experiment with floral pieces (best for special occasions, unless you're using artificial flowers). And Christmas-themed figurines or plates make quite an impact when showcased in a tree or window. Try placing lit tabletop decorations on mantels or in the center of your tree: use your imagination and experiment!

Securing pieces

Place pieces deep enough into the tree so that they'll be fully supported and won't fall. Avoid placing very large or heavy pieces at or near the top of the tree, especially on artificial trees, which won't be able to support the weight. Light, tall, and narrow pieces may be set, albeit sparingly, on the top third of the tree. If you're featuring several pieces, place the smaller ones near the top and the larger pieces near the bottom. Try to avoid placing anything on the bottommost branches, or the tree will look unbalanced. Small pieces may be hung with ornament hooks. Large pieces should be firmly attached with floral wire or fishing line (monofilament) or placed on several flattened branches that can serve as a foundation (both techniques shown at right).

LIVE-TREE TIP

Live tree branches will naturally droop a little after a day or two. To compensate, either place your statement pieces higher in the tree, or watch and see if you need to adjust the height by repositioning your pieces after the tree "settles."

HANGING WITH WIRE OR MONOFILAMENT

1 Tie the floral wire or monofilament around your piece. Then make a loop with the other end of the wire or monofilament. Loop this end around a green.

2 The statement piece should be worked into the tree, not placed at branch tips, so that the branches can support the weight. It also looks better this way.

PLACING PIECES ON A FOUNDATION

1 Flatten three or four branches to create a base, then lift others up to make space. Place a piece of cardboard on the base for support and cover with cotton batting.

2 This collectible house is nestled in a snowy landscape behind a candy-cane fence. To prevent slippage, attach the house to an inner branch using floral wire.

STATEMENT PIECES GALLERY

Note: see pages 187–89 for supplier information

COLLECTIBLES

1 Collectible lit houses can be displayed in the tree as well as under it, allowing more room for Christmas presents.

FAMILY MEMORIES

2 Take a beloved personal photograph and place it in a frame that complements the theme or style of your tree.

FLOWERS & FRUIT

3 Fill a pine-cone sleigh with brightly colored fruits and flowers to create a vivid focal point for your room or tree.

4 Adding fresh-cut flowers to a tree provides interesting shapes and enticing aromas. Look for unusual vases to enhance the look.

SEASONAL ITEMS

5 Recreate a theme from a favorite story, like *The Nutcracker,* or build a miniature Christmas scene on a red-velvet stage.

6 This two-sided wooden Santa plaque is a perfect decorative accent for a country stairway or window.

7 Retro tabletop decorations like this kitschy felt-covered reindeer look cute when placed on tree branches or wreaths.

8 Flattened branches make room for tabletop pieces. This snowman fits well with frosty tree themes.

9 A novel way to display a collectible Christmas dish is to cradle it in tree branches and arrange extra lights behind it for illumination.

10 This lovely angel with movable arms can be posed to fly, pray, or even lend a hand stringing garlands. Just attach the garland's end to her hand!

11 Use an incredibly intricate wood carving like this to light up a garlanded mantelpiece, dark window, or tabletop display.

RIBBONS & BOWS

RIBBONS AND BOWS ARE VERSATILE ACCESSORIES that add depth and texture. We consider them "through-line" decorations, meaning they can tie the whole look of your tree together and, when used throughout one or more rooms, unify entire themes or color schemes. We highly recommend wired ribbon, which lets bows and ribbon patterns keep their shape. If you are using both bows and ribbon in your design, start with the overall ribboning pattern, and finish with bows.

RIBBONING STYLES

Consider your personal "fashion sense" as well as the style of the tree and its decorations when choosing ribbon. Ribbon comes in an almost limitless selection of colors and fabrics, compatible with any type of tree design—plain and multicolored, patterned and textured, even reversible. While wired ribbon is more expensive than unwired, it's well worth the price because it's much more versatile and holds its shape longer than unwired ribbon. It can twist, turn, lie flat, or make full 360-degree spirals. Wired ribbon is widely available, comes in many styles, and allows anyone to make professional-looking designs.

▲ **Green and red** Choose contrasting colors when using two ribbons to really create a standout ribbon statement. Both ribbons should complement ornament tones.

Vertical line pattern

Lines cascading down the tree give a very symmetrical look to your design. This helps tie a look together if you have many different kinds of ornaments and want to help them look coordinated. You might look for a ribbon with an image or pattern echoed on your ornaments.

ATTACHING RIBBON

Attach the ribbon loops to your tree by bending the branch around the ribbons (on an artificial tree), or with floral wire (if your tree is live).

RIBBON AMOUNT

For standard-size trees, each style (except Picture Frame, p. 152) uses about 25 yards of ribbon. Buy three 10-yard rolls or one 25-yard roll.

1 Fold the end of the ribbon over into a loop and pinch it together. Anchor the loop to the tree with floral wire or by bending a green around the bottom of the loop.

2 Make a half-loop shape with the ribbon, and anchor it to a green about a foot below the first anchor. Don't attach it at the branch tip; go in about three inches.

3 Making sure the loops are nicely rounded, continue creating loops down the length of the tree, slightly increasing the loop size as you go downward.

Starting slightly below the treetop leaves you room to add bows or another type of treetop decoration.

Finishing ends

Complete the end of each ribbon with a decorative touch. This gives your design a pretty and professional look. Using wire snips makes cutting wired ribbon a snap!

Start with clean, sharp cutting tools to prevent ragged ribbon edges.

1 Leave enough ribbon at the bottom to create a tail. Fold the end of the ribbon in half, and cut it at an angle to create an inverted "V."

2 The "V" gives the ribbon pattern a sharp, finished look, which works well on contemporary designs.

3 Alternatively, you can curl the ribbon under and let it hang. This finish looks best on Victorian designs or trees with a soft, feminine look.

4 Make three to five vertical ribbon lines around the tree, repeating steps 1–3 each time, and making sure to space evenly between lines.

Picture frame

Framing is an excellent way to draw the eye to statement pieces that you wish to showcase in your tree. You can make and use one or more frames—in many assorted shapes, including triangular (shown here), square, diamond, and rectangular—depending on how many special items you wish to highlight. However, with this pattern, less is definitely more. Leave enough room for your piece to fit inside the "ribbon frame" without looking too cramped; leave at least several inches of space between the item and the ribbon. Once you have the spacing, measure out enough ribbon to make the frame. The amount of ribbon depends on the size of the item you're showcasing and what shape frame you want to use.

FRESH RIBBON

Before adding ribbon, place and plug in lit statement pieces, to avoid ribbon wrinkling when you snake the cord through the tree.

This snowman fits his frame well. He is placed so that the space between him and the ribbon is fairly equal all the way around.

1 Start a roll of ribbon near the treetop and attach it to a green. Then, using the looping technique shown for the Vertical Line Pattern (pages 150–51), create the first diagonal line of the triangle. Next, make the bottom, horizontal portion of the triangle. Then continue the same piece of ribbon back up to meet the green where you began your pattern. Cut the ribbon and secure.

2 Place your statement piece in the ribbon frame (if you haven't done so already) using the attachment methods outlined in Statement Pieces (pages 148–49). Repeat the Picture Frame ribbon treatment around the tree if you're using more than one statement piece.

Use bows in contrasting colors or picks (branch-tip accessories), especially at corners, to accent your frame.

Freeform

Freeforming is a great way to save money—you can use one or more types of complementary ribbons and make use of scraps you may have left over from package wrapping. By cutting ribbon into different lengths and randomly placing the strips about your tree in half-loop patterns, you create the illusion of having swirled ribbons on your tree—at a fraction of the cost.

Apply this ribbon style after your tree has been fully decorated, so you can place strips wherever you see a "hole."

1 Cut the ribbon into strips long enough to create half-loops, or gather together leftover scraps of sufficient length. Place each loop deep enough into the tree to stay in place, and hide the ends.

2 Continue randomly around the tree, using small, medium, and large loops. Using smaller pieces near the top helps keep your tree proportions balanced.

3 Loop placement is freeform, and depends on where you want to fill a space.

Wraparound

Wraparound ribboning that spirals diagonally down and around gives more of a sweeping feel to your tree, and if you add bows, it mimics the look of a ball gown. This style is slightly more formal in appearance than the Vertical-Line ribboning pattern. You can also accent this pattern with an ascending or descending parade of ornaments. Display a set of collectible train pieces "chugging" up the tree, or a series of sled ornaments "sliding" down.

Whenever you use two different ribbons, make sure they are the same width and that the materials are of similar weight. Then choose any complementary colors, patterns, or textures.

1 Lay the two different ribbons one on top of the other. Fold the doubled ends over to create a loop. Attach the doubled loop to the treetop by bending a green over it, then pull it slightly apart.

2 Continuing diagonally, make a half-loop with the two ribbons and anchor it. Spread the ribbons apart so they curve out and you can see space between them.

3 Keep spiraling down and around the tree and attaching the ribbons with tree greens. The loops may very gradually increase in size as you progress down and around the tree.

4 Finish the tail off by cutting inverted "Vs" into each ribbon end, as shown at right. Above, the fully ribboned tree is now complete and ready to be decorated with ornaments.

BOW STYLES

Bows add bright, decorative bursts of color and texture to your tree. The 3-D quality of bow loops gives the eye "stopping points" as it travels around the tree.

Use four-loop bows made of lightweight materials as accents at points of attachment along ribboning patterns. Pom-pom bows look great on a tree with ribboning, or by themselves on a tree, green garland, or wreath.

Bob's easy pom-pom bow

Bob never had much patience for following step-by-step directions, so he developed his own short-cut method for making pom-pom bows.

We don't recommend this technique for thicker ribbons like brocades or velvets, but it works well for lightweight and pliable ribbons made from fabrics such as satin and silk.

ADDED DECORATION

Try adding a "pick" (stemmed decoration) to the center of your bow for extra pizzazz and color.

RIBBON AMOUNTS

You need about 3 yards for both Bob's Easy Pom-Pom Bow and Debi's Full Pom-Pom Bow.

1 Make a loop and hold it between your thumb and index finger. Leave enough ribbon to create a tail.

2 Continue to make loops until you have enough to create a full bow; between 11 and 19 is best.

3 Pinch the bases of the ribbon loops tight, then wrap snugly several times with medium-gauge floral wire (or a pipe cleaner).

4 Twist the floral wire or pipe cleaner to secure. Leave enough floral wire untwisted to allow you to attach the bow to your greenery.

5 You may want to add a pick to your bow. Insert the pick end into the center of your unfluffed bow. Be sure it is secure within the floral-wire wrap.

6 To fluff the bow, round each loop and twist it at the bottom of the loop. Move loops around so they aren't all angled in the same direction.

7 Attach your bow to the tree with floral wire. Make any necessary adjustments to the picks, loops, and tails so the loops are rounded and the tails hang freely.

Debi's full pom-pom bow

This bow incorporates the "half-twist-between-every-loop" technique. The advantage to this method is that the neck area in the center of the bow is quite narrow; thus when you secure it with floral wire, you're assured that the loops won't slip and the bow will keep its shape. This is especially helpful if your ribbon is slippery or heavy.

1 Reversible or double-sided ribbon is ideal for this bow. Allow about 1–2 feet of ribbon for a tail, and give the ribbon a half-twist.

2 Make the first loop, and then give the ribbon another half-twist. Make a second loop and give the ribbon yet another half-twist.

3 Continue making loops, being sure to make half-twists between every loop. Make enough loops to create a full-looking bow, about 15–21 altogether. Wrap the bow with floral wire, then twist it to secure.

4 Fluff the bow, then attach it to your tree with the floral wire. Once the bow is in place, fluff all the loops so they are fully rounded. Position the tail to hang freely.

Two-ribbon pom-pom bow

Using two ribbons to make a bow is tricky and may take some practice, but it does enable you to create a full swirl of color, form, and texture. Two-ribbon bows add panache to a tree and should be prominently featured; they look best on taller, fuller trees. For beginners, sheer, lightweight ribbon is easier to shape. Use three to five yards of each of the two ribbons for this bow.

RIBBON WEIGHT

Bows made out of heavier ribbon should be placed deeper in the tree for support, and so they're better "anchored."

1 Select two identical-width ribbons of similar-weight material and in complementary colors and/or patterns. Leave about two feet on both ends for long tails.

2 Lay the ribbons one on top of the other. Holding tightly, give both ribbons a half-twist to make the first loop. Follow steps 1–4 in full pom-pom bow demo above.

3 When fluffing this bow, pull the inner loop out and twist slightly to fill any spaces. Take turns pulling the inner loops to the left and right of the outer loop, so that colors alternate.

4 Finish all tails with an inverted-"V" cut, and attach the bow to your tree with floral wire. Make a half-loop on each long ribbon end, angle it diagonally, and attach it with a green. This is an ideal bow for filling empty spaces on a tree.

Four-loop bow

These clean-looking bows provide light, gentle touches of color to a tree, and they work especially well on smaller trees. Scaled-down versions of the bows make great decorations for tabletop-sized trees without overpowering them. This style is best suited for light and narrow ribbons. If you're making small bows, use very narrow ribbon.

To make a four-loop bow with a long, trailing tail, you need less than two yards of ribbon. With such a simple bow, it is important that the ribbon looks evenly spaced. A simple trick for making similar-sized loops is to use the spacing between your index finger and thumb as a makeshift measuring tool!

1 Leaving enough ribbon for a tail, grasp the ribbon and give it a half-twist to start your first loop. Pinch either side of the twist tightly between your thumb and index finger.

2 Create your first loop, holding the ribbon between your index and middle fingers. Don't crimp it!

3 With your other hand, give the ribbon another half-twist. Now pinch the entire loop between your thumb and index finger.

4 Make a second loop. Give the ribbon another half-twist. Grasp it firmly between your thumb and index finger.

5 Make the third and fourth loops, then secure the bow at the center with floral wire. Leave enough wire untwisted to attach the bow to the tree.

6 Make a smaller fifth loop and wrap with the wire. Pull the wire back, out of the way of the loops and the tail. Fluff the bow.

7 Attach the bow to your tree with the floral wire. Fluff again if necessary.

CREATIVE USE OF RIBBONS & BOWS

Because contemporary ribbons are of much better quality than the old paper ribbons of the past, they can be used more creatively as decorative design elements. Use four-loop bows to accent interesting architectural features in your home. Use short lengths of ribbon as tiebacks for draperies. Make pom-pom bows and attach them to gifts that won't be wrapped—large children's toys like bicycles and scooters. We've even seen oversized ribbons that were used to "wrap" automobiles! Give someone the gift of flowers, and add a bow you've made for them. And outdoor ribbon-and-bow treatments can enhance doors, trees, lampposts, gates, and fences.

▶ **Lamp bow** In warm, dry climates, even rich velvet ribbons can be used to decorate outdoor light fixtures.

▲ **Electric ribbon** Lit ribbon allows you to both light and decorate. Drape it on your tree and tie it into a top bow.

OUTDOOR RIBBON

For outdoor decorating, use ribbons specially made to withstand the elements. Plastics, lamés, and even leathers, endure better than velours and delicate fabrics.

▲ **Alcove accent** Beribboned garlands aren't just for stairways and windows. Draw attention to small, decorative areas like this alcove by framing them with lit garland accented with bows.

◀ **Gold cascade** For a loose, freeform design, combine bows and draped fabric to complement ornaments and statement pieces.

GIFTWRAP

Instead of always wrapping presents in Christmas paper, try placing your gift in fabric. Gather the ends together and tie it up with some wired ribbon.

◀ **Spiral design** Swirl ribbon around and around draped green garland for an exciting, lavish look.

RIBBONS

Ribbons and bows were not a part of early Christmas decoration in Germany, where the first Christmas trees were designed. Until the 19th century, silk and velvet ribbon was reserved for the clothing of nobility; ribbon was so popular that it festooned the hairstyles, hats, dresses, jackets, and shoes of the European aristocracy. In the Victorian era, people began to attach ribbons and bows to their Christmas trees as well. Velvet, considered especially luxurious, was a popular trimming material in Victorian England, and later in America.

We still decorate our Christmas trees with ribbons and bows, as well as our Christmas presents! Now bows are made from a wide variety of fabrics, in many different colors and styles, and with the introduction of plastics, leathers and metals, many ribbons are able to endure harsh outdoor-weather conditions.

Silk, satin & nylon

Silks and satins are lightweight, and they have a light, ethereal look as well. They can be textured, like silk dupiones, or shiny and sleek like polished satins. Use these when you want to create a crisp, sharp ribbon statement. Nylon ribbons are also light. They cost less than silks and satins, but they don't provide quite the same richness. All three materials work well with most bow and ribboning styles.

Velvet & velveteen

Velvets have long been associated with nobility, and they still lend a regal air to Christmas greenery. These ribbons are plush in appearance and add a rich, upscale quality to decorations. Silk velvet is among the most expensive of all ribbons on the market, but the sophisticated look it provides is well worth the cost. Velvet ribbons made from cotton or rayon are almost as rich as silk and slightly less expensive. Cotton velveteen is the most inexpensive velvet, but it can make a fine substitute. Burgundy and green velvets look spectacular in Victorian settings.

Novelty

Novelty ribbons are made of unusual fabrics or materials designed with a unique twist. These ribbons are great for creating a theme or setting a tone. Stretch-terrycloth ribbons, which are reminiscent of beach towels, can be used with electric ribbon to create a beach-themed design. Faux-fur ribbons and animal ornaments make excellent pet or wildlife trees. And there's even something for motorcycle enthusiasts: black leather ribbon, with or without zippers!

RIBBON & BOW GALLERY

Note: see pages 187–89 for supplier information.

SILK, SATIN & NYLON

1 Red and chartreuse silk dupione with gold edging

2 Satiny sheer, pastel blue with gold edging

3 Satiny, translucent fuchsia with gold edging

VELVET & VELVETEEN

4 Black burnout velvet with leaves edged in gold

5 Teal lamé with black burnout velvet and gold glitter

6 Maroon velvet with gold-beaded edging

7 Jewel-tone velvet harlequin

8 Two-sided maroon velveteen with gold, hot-drop metal

9 Green velvet ribbon with embroidered gold crests

10 Black velveteen with sequined diamond shapes and gold piping on edges

NOVELTY

11 Hot-pink stretch terry-cloth

12 Black faux leather with gold rickrack

13 Gold-on-gold faux sequins

14 Reptile-patterned gray latex

15 Gold wire mesh

16 Tan leather with gold, hot-drop metal, and black stitching

17 Crimped red lamé with gold edging

18 Two-sided black polyblend and gold lamé

19 Faux snow leopard with black leather edging

20 Hot-pink leather with black stitching

21 Indoor/outdoor teal vinyl

22 Red velvet with metal jingle-bell accents

FABRIC

LIKE RIBBON, FABRIC CAN BE USED as an element
to tie together the colors in the room with the
colors you choose for your tree trimmings. Since
fabric is fuller than ribbon, it looks best on trees
that aren't too bushy. It also works well to fill
space if you don't have many ornaments
or decorations for your tree.

SUITABLE MATERIALS

It's best to use brightly colored fabric, as dark colors tend
to get lost in the green of the tree. Use lightweight
materials like satin, tulle, lamé, or moiré. Although thick,
heavy fabrics can help create a spectacular display, they
don't drape well and can cause tree branches to droop,
so use them sparingly. If you do use a heavy fabric like
faux fur, as we did on the Mae West tree (opposite
page, inset), let it hang straight down.

Fabric flowerette

Instead of adding ribbon bows to a tree draped in fabric,
you could create one or more flowers from the draping fabric.
They can be used at the treetop as the starting point for your
drape, or placed throughout the tree.

> **FABRIC ALLOWANCE**
>
> Use two yards of fabric per
> foot of tree. Allow up to 10
> more for a draped tree skirt.

▲ **Couture** Here, two different fabrics were
overlapped and styled to create the impression that
the tree is actually "dressed."

1 Choose a fabric that complements the color of your
tree decorations. Fold over about one foot of
fabric—by doubling the material, you can create
soft, rounded "rose petals." Start a rosette by curling the
doubled material around into a spiral.

2 Tighten the spiral on the rosette. Firmly grasp
the finished "flowerette" about six to eight
inches from the top. You may want to wrap it
with floral wire to prevent the fabric from shifting; this
is especially helpful with slippery fabrics like satin.

3 Attach the flowerette to the treetop by bending
several greens around it. Once it has been secured,
open the "petals" of the flowerette by shaping the
fabric. If you're just creating flowerettes for the tree, cut
the fabric. If you're continuing with loops, go on to step 4.

FABRIC GALLERY

1 Synthetic metallic gold
2 Sheer red tulle with blue sequins
3 White silk dupione
4 Gold and saffron chiffon
5 Faux leopard-spotted acetate
6 Sequined silver nylon
7 Turquoise satin
8 Hand-stitched ivory sequins on sheer fabric
9 White faux fur
10 Red velvet

LARGE-BULB FABRIC SAFETY

If you use this technique on a tree lit with large C-7 or C-9 bulbs, keep fabric away from the warm bulbs. If the fabric needs to be attached near a bulb to accomodate your design, cheat! Unscrew the bulb until it is no longer lit.

Notice that the rose is angled up. Don't let it droop and weigh down your design.

▲ **Mae West homage tree**
Since this tree was an ode to excess, we bunched heavy faux fur to frame the tree and allowed it to flow to the floor.

4 Create "loops" on the tree, in much the same way as shown in the Vertical Line Pattern ribbon demonstration on pages 150–51. Anchor the loops by bending greens around the fabric. Make sure the fabric loops are full and billowy by fluffing them out when all of the fabric is attached.

5 Let the fabric drape down to the floor, and create your tree skirt by surrounding the tree stand with fabric. Finish by folding under all unfinished ends to give the skirt a soft, rounded look.

GARLANDS

GARLANDS, LIKE MOST OTHER TREE DECORATIONS, come in a variety of styles. They can be made of plastic, paper, glass, metal, ceramic, and even food. Many ornament manufacturers even make matching or complementary garlands to go with their ornaments.

HANGING PATTERNS

There are several different ways to hang bead, pearl, and novelty garlands. Note that if you choose a symmetrical garland pattern for your tree, you should hang them before adding ornaments so the garlands will hang as evenly as possible. It's easier to hang ornaments around garlands than to look for an available branch after you've hung an ornament on every single tree branch. For those of you with pets—especially cats—you may want to rethink using garland at all. One good swat and it's goodbye garland. (And your pet probably won't be too thrilled if the tree topples its way.)

Metallic or tinsel garlands have been used over the years to decorate trees, stairways, windows, lampposts, mailboxes, and even work cubicles. Invariably, tinsel garland used to be attached with cellophane tape, but now, a variety of attachment devices are available, including plastic hooks with two-sided tape, floral wire and even Velcro.

Tuck pattern

Tinsel garlands work well on both live and artificial trees because they are lightweight. Instead of looping this garland in the "Wedding Cake" pattern (see next page), try tucking it a little deeper into the tree. This gives the design more depth, and the light reflected off the shimmery garland actually bounces more light off your ornaments and makes them brighter. Don't hang ornaments off decorative garland since it is so light that the ornaments might pull the garland off the tree! The only exception is our sturdy Charm Bracelet garland (see page 164). For a seven-foot-tall tree, use eight to ten strands of six-foot-long-tinsel garland.

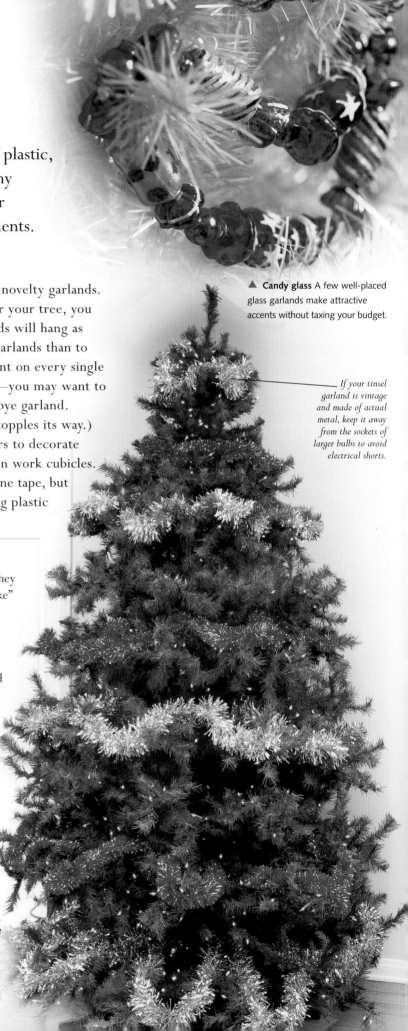

▲ **Candy glass** A few well-placed glass garlands make attractive accents without taxing your budget.

If your tinsel garland is vintage and made of actual metal, keep it away from the sockets of larger bulbs to avoid electrical shorts.

1 Start at the bottom of the tree. Lay garland along the branch, "tucking" it into the tree and creating "U" shapes. At the end of one garland, start another.

2 After finishing the first row of branches, move up to the next row. The completed tree should look like it's covered in soft ruffles. Decrease loop size slightly as you move up.

Wedding cake pattern

One of the most familiar patterns—where garlands are strung symmetrically in tiers—"Wedding Cake" works well with almost any type of bead garland. The spacing must be done evenly to look right. It is more difficult to drape on a live tree since the branches are random shapes and lengths. Since garlands should be hung near branch tips, use lightweight garlands on live trees or your branches will droop. If the garlands slip when they're draped over branches, you may want to attach them with floral wire or ornament hooks. For a seven-foot-tall tree, use between eight and ten strands of bead-chain garland. These usually come in lengths of nine feet.

For shorter rows, you can tuck the garland into the tree or tie it into a knot if you don't want to cut it short.

Use garland of a single color and bead size or any combination of colors and bead sizes.

You can "cheat" by using ornament hooks or floral wire to make the garlands hang exactly where you want them.

1 Start at the bottom of the tree. Attach the first garland to an artificial green (by bending it around the garland), or to a live branch (with floral wire).

2 A more decorative way to start and end each garland is by tying the beads around the green and making a knot.

3 Drape the garland horizontally over branches, creating a loose loop pattern. When you finish looping one garland, attach another. After completing one row, move up to the next.

4 Decrease loop width slightly as you move up the tree. Here, every row was garlanded. You may also choose to hang beads only on every other row.

Charm bracelet

Are you worried that your garlands are too thin and insignificant? Try our "Charm Bracelet" solution. You can create a flashy charm bracelet for your tree by twisting several garlands together and attaching small ornaments every few inches with ornament hooks, or try the special technique demonstrated below. The Charm Bracelet garland looks best hung symmetrically, with a mix of beads in different sizes and colors.

1 Make a knot with three to five garlands, twist them together, and hang the knotted end off of a high green. Drape the garland around the tree using Wedding Cake or Random Swag method.

2 Once the garland is hung, begin adding the "charm" ornaments. First, pop the metal legs out of the crown of the ornament and slip the metal piece over a bead strand.

3 Position the ornament under the legs, replace the crown, and insert the legs back into the ornament. Add an ornament about every eight to ten inches. Use a few different styles and shapes.

Random swag

Another option is a random pattern, which involves many strands of garlands and careful, patient work. Although it's called random, the garlands must be placed carefully so they aren't too tightly or loosely draped. Drape garlands diagonally from branch row to branch row, many times, crossing strands over one another. This pattern will give your tree a drippy, ornate look.

Random patterns looks best with small glass-bead garlands.

Leave the top of the tree unbeaded to save room for your treetop design.

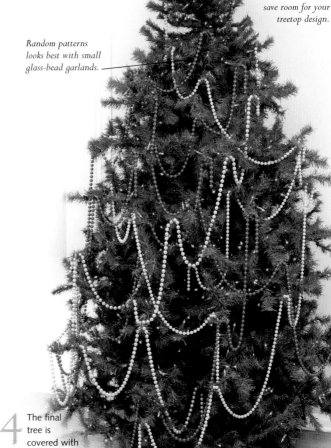

1 Make an irregular loop with one type of bead garland and drape it over a high branch. Continue looping over branches at random heights. Don't make the loops too tight.

2 Repeat with a separate color or style of bead garland, crisscrossing them and varying the shape of the loops.

3 Create visual diversity by varying how many branches you skip to form loops. Avoid making a symmetrical pattern.

4 The final tree is covered with garlands crisscrossing every which way.

DECORATING WITH GARLANDS

Garlands can be used inside or outside, to embellish fireplaces, to frame windows and doorways, to dress up a buffet table, or to wrap a mailbox or lamppost. Bead chains can be hung alone on the wall or added to a tree, wreath, or green garland. Floral garlands look great when laid on top of green garlands and accented with ornaments. Make a table-centerpiece garland by cutting a piece of green garland, tying the ends together, and placing a decorative piece in the center. Fluff any bushy garlands well before adding lights or decorations.

▲ Dressing up
Adding an upscale bead chain to a green garland dresses it up considerably.

◀ Bridge the gap
Unite a tree with its environs by hanging matching garland along the windows.

▼ Stone fireplace
This commanding feature required decorations that were large and substantial.

▲ Draped glamour
Multiple layers of bead chain look dramatic on a wall. Metal architectural elements make natural hooks for this elegant garland.

▶ Limited space
Frame a window in your kitchen to tie in with decorations in the rest of the house.

▼ Suede greens
A piece of greenery and a few ornaments on your table dress up place settings. This suede garland looks live, but doesn't leave needles or sap.

GARLAND STYLES

Garlands have been used as celebratory embellishments since Roman times, when they were used to deck doors and walls during festivals. The tradition continued into the Middle Ages, when Germans hung wooden hoops decorated with boughs as symbols of good luck at Christmastime. The Germans were also the first to trim their Christmas trees with glass-bead garlands, in the 17th century, and with silver tinsel garland in the late 1800s. The Victorians strung their trees with glass beads, berries, and paper. Garlands have evolved in contemporary times; today you can find contemporary fluffy tinsel in a rainbow of colors, and strung garlands made of everything from popcorn to plastic to fine crystal.

Plastic

Plastic garlands can be safely used either indoors or out. They are inexpensive and have greater durability than their more expensive and fragile glass counterparts, and they come in an even broader range of shapes, from simple beads to freeform acrylic to the most fanciful forms imaginable.

Craft / Natural

Beads made of colored wood and fabric have a country feel, and they work well on floral-themed trees. Everyone remembers making rings out of colored aluminum ribbon or construction paper; this retro look is fun and easy to make at home (although preassembled metallic rings are available in stores). Classic popcorn and berry garlands are also do-it-yourself nostalgic looks. You can buy garlands made of twigs and pinecones to add texture and a nice rustic accent. Green garland will never go out of style, and you can choose from a myriad of live or artificial needles.

Glass

The variety of glass garland is limitless—there are styles and colors to suit any type of tree or theme. You can find classic round beads, abstract shapes, novelty shapes, and luxurious crystal.

Tinsel / Fashion

In 19th-century Germany, tinsel garland was made from real silver—contemporary versions are made from new flame- and tarnish-proof materials and come in a wide variety of bright, shiny colors. "Fashion" garlands are artificial branch-style garlands made of PVC (polyvinyl chloride) in colors other than green, such as white, black, pastels, and many color combinations.

GARLAND GALLERY

Note: see pages 187–89 for supplier information.

PLASTIC & STYROFOAM

1 Miniature mirrored-acrylic "disco" balls linked by tiny silver beads

2 Purple hearts and clear, blue, fuchsia, gold, and red shatter-proof multishaped beads

3 Red, white, and pearl triple bead strands

4 Acrylic "ice" chips on silver wire

5 Round and faceted beads in gold, copper, and burgundy

6 Gold-tone metal bells on red-and-crystal bead chain

7 Vintage white plastic lanterns with holly accents on white chain

8 Frosted Styrofoam berries on a branch

CRAFT / NATURAL

9 Retro metallic-ribbon chain links

10 Twig garland with pinecones

11 Felt bead chain in shades of blue, gray, and beige

12 Wooden C-9 light bulbs on corkscrew wire

GLASS

13 Upscale beads and candy chain

14 Matte-finish jewel-tone beads

15 Lemon-and-lime chain with semi-matte finish

16 Small, shiny faceted and round beads in jewel tones

17 Upscale retro ornamental beads

18 Sunflowers with varied bead shapes and colors

ORNAMENTS

THE EARLIEST CHRISTMAS-TREE ORNAMENTS were paper flowers, fruit, and sweets. The 16th-century Germans decorated their fir trees with these elements to symbolize the Tree of Knowledge in the Garden of Eden. Soon after, German markets began to offer painted or gilded wax ornaments, usually shaped into angels, during Christmas fairs. Victorian trees were decorated with foodstuffs, including sugared nuts, sweets, and local fruit; and ornaments ranging from intricately cut paper or crocheted snowflakes, to handmade wood and tin figures, to glass ornaments imported from Germany.

BLOWN GLASS

Europeans are still practicing the ancient art of glass-blowing, a technique discovered in the 1st century BC by the Phoenicians. The first glass-blown Christmas ornaments appeared in the 17th century in Bohemia (now the Czech Republic) and Germany; they were created as an afterwork pastime by glassblowers.

Queen Victoria first imported glass ornaments from Germany in the 1850s, making them fashionable throughout England. In 1880, F. W. Woolworth began to import glass ornaments to the United States to sell in his numerous stores. By 1890, he was importing more than 200,000 ornaments annually.

The ornament starts its life as a hot, molten globe of glass. The molten glass is mouth-blown by a craftsperson or machine-blown in a factory. After an ornament is blown and shaped, it is left clear or "silvered," which involves pouring silver nitrate into the interior of the piece and swirling it to coat and strengthen it. The ornament is then handpainted, dipped in paint, or sprayed, making every ornament unique. Finally, glitter can be added.

OTHER GLASS TECHNIQUES

There are other techniques that produce exceptional styles and shapes of glass Christmas decorations, too. Stained-glass pieces create a beautiful glow when they are hung and lit properly, and exquisite handcut Austrian crystal pieces lend a touch of glittering class to a tree.

BLOWN-GLASS GALLERY

Note: see pages 187–89 for supplier information.

1 Lime-green ball with handpainted red poinsettias

2 Red-and-green-striped handpainted ball

3 Frosty pink egg with pink floral-glitter design

4 Long, tapering copper drop with paint-and-glitter highlights

5 Etched Egyptian glass with 18-carat-gold highlights

6 Etched Egyptian glass with 18-carat-gold highlights and burgundy-tinted bands

7 Clear bell with white snow-scape and 18-carat-gold accents

8 Red balls handpainted with paisley motif

9 Gold drop with handpainted Three Wise Men

10 White frosty ball with handpainted pussywillows

11 Blue-tinted etched Egyptian glass with 18-carat-gold highlights and oblong drop

12 Red ball with handpainted white lilies

13 Pale peach ball with handpainted contemporary floral pattern

14 Clear ball with handpainted red-orange tulips

15 Red egg with handpainted golden pears

16 White ball with pink glitter roses and pink rose-ball drop

17 Blue-tinted etched Egyptian glass with 18-carat-gold highlights and crystal drop

18 Pointed frosted teardrop with tinted translucent floral design and gold glitter

19 Zebra-patterned ball with gold flecks

20 Ruby-red traditional ball with shiny leaf pattern and ball-drop accent

21 Clear ball with 18-carat-gold swirl stripes

22 Bronze ball with ornate floral-motif glittered paint

23 Green ball with gold mottling and green feather accent

OTHER GLASS TECHNIQUES

24 Flat fusion-glass ball ornament with stars and stripes

25 Silver-wire heart with clear faceted beads and ribbon tie

26 Silver spiky diamond shape with stained-glass look

27 Medium-sized stained-glass Santa window decoration

MOLDED GLASS

The practice of creating molded-glass objects dates back to ancient Egypt. Contemporary developments in glass-molding techniques allow artists to create complicated and highly sculptural designs. First, the glass artist creates a drawing of his vision. Then a sculptor creates a 3-D clay mold of the design, so that glass can be poured in and take on the same form. When the glass cools, the mold, which is made of two halves, is opened and removed, and what remains is clear glass in the shape of the original design. Silvering, painting, and glittering complete the process. Illustrated here are just a few of the molded-glass ornaments created by modern artists and companies.

Ornament hangers

Ornament style dictates ornament-hanger type: some ornaments come with their own ribbons or cords. Retro designs should hang from classic metal hooks, while designer glass and crystal pieces demand upscale hangers. For heavy and collectible pieces, two hooks are safer.

1. Ribbons and braided cords are old-style ornament hangers.

2. Simple metal hooks work, but they can scratch ornaments.

3. Coated metal hooks cause less damage to fine glass pieces.

4. Plastic hooks are great: they're safe to store on fine collectibles.

5. Designer hooks may include clear or tinted crystals.

6. Springy, expandable hangers help with ornament placement.

Securing ornament crowns

Make sure that crowns on collectibles or pricey ornaments are secure before hanging them. Loose crowns can be secured with a drop or two of glue. An alternative fix is demonstrated below (protect your hands by applying hand lotion before using a glue gun). Serious collectors may not want to do either, since altering the ornament will lessen its value.

1 Carefully remove the crown from the neck of the ornament. Spread the legs of the insertion wires apart.

2 Gently insert the legs halfway back in. Add a dab or two of hot glue to the rim of the open ornament.

3 Gently push the crown down until it's firmly in place. If any glue seeps out, remove it with a toothpick. Let dry.

MOLDED-GLASS GALLERY

Note: see pages 187–89 for supplier information.

1 Two-piece red bikini molded onto miniature gold wire hangers

2 Red reindeer with gold glittered antlers and feet

3 White teapot with delicate pink-rose pattern

4 Gold angel in flight with horn and banner

5 Red London-style telephone booth with silvered-glass panels

6 Spiky, glittered glass icicle twist in bright jewel tones

7 Cheery yellow duck pull-toy on wagon with button wheels

8 Four-piece blue train set with glitter "steam" and details

9 Bright-red cardinal seated on a leafy branch

10 Tropical island sunset hand-painted on a Hawaiian shirt

11 Gold-and-white cross with faux-jewel accents

12 Handpainted egg with ocean scene and raised palm fronds

13 Deep blue Star of David with gold-glitter edging

14 Delicately molded green leaf with gold-glitter veins and stem

15 Handpainted, glittered clip-on hummingbird in midflight

16 Gold camel with purple saddle and yellow rope reins

17 Maple leaf "cookie" with orange frosting and white glitter

18 White-glittered heart with red AIDS-Awareness ribbon

19 Green-clad boy, with scarf and hat, making a snow angel

20 Spiky-bottomed jewel-tone drop with glittery patterns

21 Vintage-looking glittery gold Father Christmas with tiny tree

22 Reproduction of a sock monkey doll, holding a banana

23 Festive heart-shaped sweet with waffle pattern

24 Retro-style pink-and-blue striped ball with sunburst cutout

25 Blue, white, and gold Star of David and dreidel

26 Frosted red heart with a shiny indent edged in gold glitter

27 Sexy leopard-print dress molded onto a gold hanger

28 Pink patchwork quilted tree for Breast Cancer Awareness

29 Roly-poly snowman outfitted for snow removal

30 Three nested bells with candy-cane motif

31 Glittered gingerbread man with mittens, earmuffs, and wreath

32 Blue-and-gold miniature replica of the Eiffel Tower

33 Bright gold lion with faux-ruby eyes

34 Exotic fish in brilliant tropical colors

35 Multifaceted silver star with glittered edging

36 "Christmas pickle," a German family tradition

37 Red glittered fire engine with gold ladder

PORCELAIN

Porcelain ornaments are finely crafted ceramic pieces with a translucent quality. The handpainted and white drop-shaped ones that we used throughout this book project a delicate femininity that's perfect for Victorian or all-white design themes.

RESIN

Solid ornaments of resin are substantially more durable than lightweight hollow plastic and delicate glass baubles. They are produced by pouring resin into carved molds and are then painted and glazed.

METAL

Silver, gold, copper, brass, and tin are all used in ornament design. Metal ornaments range from whimsical miniature tin sculptures, to flat metal-beaded shapes, to exquisitely crafted upscale sterling-silver or gold sculptural pieces.

WOOD

Carved wooden pieces lean toward the whimsical side of the ornament spectrum. Whether plain, lacquered, or painted, wooden ornaments look best on country- and children's-themed trees.

PLASTIC

With innovations in manufacturing, some plastic ornaments now look as expensive and pretty as glass ones. Their advantages are lower price, lighter weight, and durability.

FABRIC

Fabric ornaments are lightweight and durable. Handcrafted dolls, toy-inspired characters, and felt decorations are appropriate for retro or children's trees, while elegant Styrofoam balls covered in fabric and decorated with piping, ribbon, and beads complement upscale trees, whether Victorian, Traditional, or Jewel-Tone.

FOOD

Home-baked cookies, store-bought candies, and even citrus peels crafted into figurines lend a warm, homey feeling to your tree. Your food ornaments can be reused from year to year—simply store them in an airtight container.

PAPER

Photographs and drawings, origami shapes, and cutout snowflakes are perennial favorites. Pictures of family and friends make great party conversation pieces. Keep paper ornaments away from larger bulbs.

GALLERY OF OTHER MATERIALS

Note: see pages 187–89 for supplier information.

PORCELAIN
1. White porcelain pointed drop with raised white pattern
2. White porcelain ball with white raised poinsettia and holly

RESIN
3. Vintage sleigh with girl in red
4. Brightly colored hot-air balloon
5. Antique toy spinner with Santa in center
6. Gold leaf on gold resin harp
7. Beaded circle with quatrefoil design in the center
8. Pie-shaped potpourri-holder ornament

METAL
9. Flat, hand-beaded, decorative pewter Christmas tree
10. Distressed-tin antique toy boat
11. Red tin heart with arrow and flame
12. Art-deco sterling-silver reindeer

WOOD
13. Ribbon-wrapped straw wreath with wooden bears
14. Felt-covered Styrofoam snowman with wood-stick arms

PLASTIC
15. Purple, shatterproof, glittery pears with stems and leaves
16. Acrylic, pastel-blue snowflake
17. Lightly frosted red-berry ball with cord hanger
18. Acrylic gold crown with ruby-red-beaded drop
19. Retro kitchen appliances: iron, fan, mixer, and toaster
20. Handbeaded Mexican heart
21. Plastic red-and-gold eight-pointed star
22. Shatterproof clip-on butterfly in shades of blue
23. Acrylic red pomegranate with red crystal seeds

FABRIC
24. Gold ball with pearl-and-sequin pins and red tassel
25. Black-and-leopard ball with pearl beading and bow
26. Beige fabric ball with gold piping in Medieval pattern
27. Red brocade ball with white fur trim
28. Chartreuse felt bag with red stitching and candy-cane appliqué
29. Wood nutcracker head and torso with tassel bottom

FOOD
30. Homemade gingerbread man with icing accents
31. Red-and-white-striped candy canes
32. Orange-peel-and-rope angel with wood-ball head

PAPER
33. Paper cocktail umbrellas, shown with glass pineapple
34. Paper-fabric gold and silver leaves on inverted teardrop
35. Beige-and-cream cardboard stars with textured paint

COLLECTIBLE ORNAMENTS

ONCE PURCHASED, A COLLECTIBLE ornament continues to increase in value every year, due to limited supply, attrition due to breakage, and the frailty of ornaments in general—making the collectible-ornament business a booming industry. Ornaments in many different media have found favor with collectors. Government mints have issued gold-plated 3-D filigree pieces, retail chains release continuing series from year to year, and individual manufacturers produce ornaments in porcelain, metal, wood, resin, and of course blown and molded glass.

LIMITLESS APPEAL

There seem to be collectibles that appeal to just about everyone. Whether you are a lover of glass balls, tin trains, cut and etched crystal, carved wood, or lit and animated ornaments, there's something somewhere for you. The Internet has made access to small companies easier, and fine craftspeople capable of limited production have found a larger audience than in the past because of improved online searching and purchasing technologies.

So how do you know what is collectible? Simply put, the most important way to start a collection is by collecting ornaments that you like, without worrying about investment potential. Collecting pieces you don't like and have no interest in, simply to wait for them to appreciate in value, is no fun. Instead, look for a style, shape, or theme that you feel a real fondness for. That way you'll not only build a strong, solid collection; you'll also enjoy each and every piece along the way.

There are a few criteria that will affect collectibility: Limited editions, where a finite quantity of pieces is produced, are more valuable; the edition number should be marked on the ornament or on an accompanying certificate of authenticity. If a piece is retired from a collection and you already own it, it becomes instantly more collectible. A craftsperson's signature on an ornament provides additional value.

COLLECTIBLES GALLERY

Note: see pages 187–89 for vendor information.

1   This glass "Flower Power" van by Department 56 was a hit with lovers of automobiles from the 1970s.

2   Egyptian glass by De Elena is tinted, decoratively cut, and accented with fine gold paint.

3   An exquisite Swarovski crystal by J.P. Brown reflects the light beautifully. Accompanying crystal and metal hangers add to the upscale quality.

4   This collector-series piece from Ornaments to Remember is numbered and depicts the erupting Kilauea volcano.

5   Joy to the World, creator of this "Big Apple," donates a portion of the profits from each ornament to a charity, and each piece is championed by a celebrity spokesperson.

6   This retired piece by Polonaise was popular due its unique construction. Each glass wing was carefully attached to the dragonfly's body.

7   Series ornaments like these "12 Days of Christmas" glass balls by Abigail's Collections make a great tree theme.

8   The creator of this line, Larry Fraga Designs, is known for the whimsy of his pieces. Also, glitter plays a large part in the decorative process.

9   Each piece by Mary Margaret Cannon's Sacred Season has a spiritual significance, and some have been limited and numbered.

10 This gold reflector ball by Christopher Radko is a hand-painted reproduction of a classic Polish design.

11 Small sterling-silver ornaments, like this reindeer from Hand & Hammer Silversmiths, can also serve as jewelry or gift-box adornments.

12 This pink quilted tree by Joy to the World is dedicated to Breast Cancer Awareness.

13 This medallion by Austrian Christmas Tree, inspired by a couture-clothing designer, was chosen to grace the cover of a Barbra Streisand Christmas CD.

14 Mattarusky artist Matt Litavasky first carved this snowman ornament out of clay. It was then made into a mold, and the final piece was handpainted and glittered.

15 Each of these blown-glass wonders by Ne'Qwa is painted on the inside through the tiny opening on top.

16 A translucent piece of art by Mark Klaus; his work is highly valued for the attention to detail and intricate design of each ornament mold.

FINISHING TOUCHES

YOU CAN COMPLETE YOUR TREE by dressing it with decorative branch-tip accessories (called "picks") and glass or tinsel icicles. Picks are decorations attached to pointy stems that you simply stick into tree branches. They make colorful and textural space-fillers. Glass icicles are replicas of ice formations that hang like ornaments. In medieval times, tinsel icicles were made of hammered silver strips and draped individually onto greens; now they are made of aluminum paper. Icicles add sparkle and vertical elements to your design.

PICK & ICICLE STYLES

Icicles—both the tinsel and glass types—were a Christmas staple in the 1950s, but it seems to us that people are not quite sure what to do with picks, so here are some tips for both. Picks come in a wide variety of styles, shapes, and colors, and can be made of glass, metal, or plastic, or found in nature. Both artificial and natural shapes include everything from berries, flowers, and pinecones to birds and feathers. There are two attachment methods, depending on the pick: inserting directly, and wiring. Picks with long stems usually stay in place. Heavy picks with short stems may need to be attached with floral wire. Our unique method for attaching icicles and tinsel is demonstrated on the next page.

Inserting picks

The key to natural-looking picks is in their shaping and placement. Place picks near branch tips, on every second or third branch. Use enough picks to make an impact.

▶ **Correct placement** Insert the pick point about eight inches back on the branch, and bend it around the branch or wrap a green around the pick stem. Reshape if needed; the berries and branches should be spread out, not crushed.

NATURAL-LOOKING PICKS

Things found in nature usually look best when placed naturally—Mother Nature knows best. Place flowers in your tree so that they appear to be facing the sun, and carefully shape flower petals so they appear natural. Birds should not be hung upside down! Spend time attaching each bird securely, because the wires on their feet are prone to slide. Shape the bird's feet before wiring, so it looks like the bird is perched on a branch.

▶ **Picks alone** Bunches of artificial cherries placed in a small tabletop tree create a simple, clean design.

Wiring picks

You can make your own picks by wiring a wide variety of items. Fruits and pinecones can be attached to trees, wreaths, or garlands. Avoid using fresh fruits in very warm climates, or if you have children or pets.

WIRING PINECONES

1 Attach floral wire to the pinecone by wrapping it tightly around its wider end and twisting to secure.

2 Wire the pinecone about three to four inches from the branch tip of your tree, wreath, or garland.

WIRING FRUIT

1 Take a strong piece of floral wire and push it all the way through whatever fruit you choose to use.

2 If hanging the fruit, twist the wire above the top of the fruit. If placing it in a branch, twist at the bottom.

Glass & tinsel icicles

Icicles add long, lean lines that are nice contrasts to round ornaments and give the eye "jumping-off" points when viewing the tree's design.

GLASS ICICLES

1 Loop the icicle's string or plastic loop around a green. Then wrap several times around the green so the icicle, not the string, is featured.

2 After wrapping the string, you may need to move a green or two to allow the icicle to hang straight.

TINSEL ICICLES

▲ **Tinsel icicles** Use tinsel sparingly for a clean look. Don't throw clumps of them onto your tree. Separate the strands and place a few at a time on branches to give your tree a nice shimmery quality. You should be able to see your tree through the tinsel.

TOXIC TINSEL

Keep cats, dogs, and babies away from aluminum tinsel. It can be toxic if ingested.

Note: see pages 187–89 for vendor information.

FINISHING TOUCHES GALLERY

ARTIFICIAL PICKS

1 Silk, long-stemmed, pale gold poinsettia

2 Lightly snow-frosted plastic berries, leaves, and pinecones

3 Plastic, clear-frosted, red-berry bunch

4 Plastic bunch of gold pears and white berries with green-fabric leaves

5 Plastic bunch of gold pinecones, colored berries, and leaves

6 Molded-glass sunflowers with long, delicate stems

7 Plastic, gold-glittered quill feather with bendable wire center

NATURAL PICKS

8 Tip of a jewel-toned peacock feather

9 Pastel pink roses and lilac waxflowers

10 Flowering-kale and orange half

11 Fresh green apple pick

ICICLES

12 Molded-glass spiral-shaped icicle and purple transparent-glass icicle

TREETOPS

TREETOPS, LIKE TREE SKIRTS, help to balance your Christmas tree. The treetop is the crowning touch, but it should make a statement without overpowering your tree. If you have "themed" your tree, you should use one of the theme elements on top. Traditionalists simply place their electric angel at the top of the tree, plug her in, and are done. Crafty people might whip something together using ribbon, fabric, feathers, picks, and whatever else they have lying around. The rest of us go to the store and hunt. Luckily, you can find many things to put on top of your tree.

▲ Tree tops can be used anywhere on a tree. This beaded star is featured as a statement piece near the treetop.

TREETOP STYLES

Electrical decorations include angels, stars, and any other small pieces that would match the style of your tree. Make sure to hide the cord so the focus is the treetop, not a tangle of wire. Nonelectrical decorations include bows, picks, sprays, angels, dolls, toys, feathers, garland, fabric, picture frames, tabletop decorations, glass spires, and live and artificial flowers. You can even create special looks by removing the treetop entirely and replacing it with one large specialty piece or prop.

Multiple-element themed top

Illustrate the story of your tree theme in one eye-catching display by creating a visually interesting treetop. Try combining several elements: surround an angel with bows, group an odd number of finials, or cluster several ornaments used in your tree. Here, we mixed a gnarly tree branch with a red-berry garland and three teddy bears for a cute country look.

▲ **Multibow treetop** Instead of using only one bow on your treetop, create a superbow to add drama and form to your treetop. Attach two or three medium-sized bows around the top row of branches on your treetop, and then shape them to create the illusion of one bow. Let the tiptop green stand out above the bows.

1 Stick a bare branch into the tree. Make sure it's deep enough so that its weight is supported. Then use several pieces of floral wire to attach the branch.

2 Add berry picks or garlands to the branch. They provide bright contrasting color and match the colors in the bears' outfits.

3 Finally, position the bears along the branches. These colors and decorations should be carried down into the rest of the tree design.

Electrical treetops

Many electrical tabletop decorations make fine treetops alone or combined with other items.

1   Plug in your lit piece or pieces, hide the cords within the tree, and position into place. These lampposts were secured using the tree's greens.

2   To add a large piece such as this doll, you may have to flatten a few branches first. Then attach the doll in two places with floral wire so it will stay in place.

SIZE MATTERS

If you have a very tall or full tree, use a large treetop. Thinner, slighter trees can make do with smaller treetops. Don't use anything too heavy at the top, or your tree will look unbalanced. Whatever you choose to use, you should use floral wire to help secure the treetop to avoid any mishaps.

TREETOP GALLERY

Note: see pages 187–89 for vendor information.

1   A bouquet of fruits, berries, and sprigs of rosemary burst forth from the treetop, accented with pinecones of various sizes.

2   Angels have been treasured treetops since Victorian times. Here, three angels surround a silver starburst.

3   Using several glass-spire treetops clustered at the top of the tree makes a much more interesting design than a single spire placed alone on the top green.

4   Cover the entire treetop with wide loops of wired ribbon. Make sure the loops are twisted around to ensure there are no large gaps in the design.

5   For a spectacular headdress to cap off a tree inspired by Mae West, we placed large, fluffy ostrich feathers in red, white, and black into the treetop.

6   This large, lit treetop star was used on the front of the tree near the very top, but not attached to the topmost green. Display heavy pieces slightly lower than the top of the tree to avoid top-heaviness.

7   Electric ribbon, which is actually a light set enclosed in clear ribbon made from PVC and tinted in bright colors, can be tied into a bow and used alone as a lit treetop.

8   Three different treetop stars were attached in a vertical line, and a wired ribbon bow was attached behind them to serve as a decorative background.

9   This collectible doll was used in place of the green treetop. The dress holds her in place, and at its base we placed ribbon rolled into tight loops to create the illusion of a ruffled crinoline.

10   We draped the neck of this mannequin head in fabric to create the top of a dress and then used a pearl garland as an elegant necklace. We placed glittering stars around her head at different levels to complete the fashion statement.

TREE SKIRTS

THERE ARE MANY VARIETIES of tree skirt on the market, from traditional 1950s felt cutouts, to waterproof plastic rounds, to elegant and upscale satins, silks, and brocades.

You should place something around the bottom of your tree for several reasons. The most practical reason is to hide your tree stand. From a fashion standpoint, the tree skirt "grounds" your Christmas tree. It finishes off the look of the tree the way accessories in fashion complement an outfit. It also balances your tree. Most trees are so covered in decorations that they can look top-heavy without a skirt. Finally, if your carpet or flooring is not of a complementary color to your tree, the fabric between it and the tree serves as a color buffer zone and blends everything together. Remember—your tree's not fully dressed without a skirt.

▲ **Decorative motifs** Patterned tree skirts can help continue your design theme to the tree's base. Here, the snowy theme was boldly emblazoned on the skirt with festive snowflakes that brighten up the shadowy areas under the tree.

◀ **Good coverage** Make sure that your tree skirt is wide enough to extend beyond the longest lower branches, so that it can be seen. Otherwise, by the time you finish decorating your tree and adding houses, nativities, a train, and packages, the skirt will be completely covered.

▲ **Choosing colors** Tree skirts should contain one or more of the colors used on your tree, or complement the tree's colors by providing a nice contrast. The skirt should not overpower the tree: here, the vivid jewel-toned ornaments are able to stand up to the fuchsia skirt, which would be too overwhelmingly bright for softer-toned themes. Generally, avoid dark-colored fabrics, since the tree casts a shadow.

SKIRTS FOR LIVE TREES

Live tree trunks have larger diameters than the metal poles of artificial trees, so make sure the tree-skirt opening is large enough. Keep the skirt out of the tree stand to avoid water damage (or use a water-resistant fabric). Launder your skirt before storage.

Fabric tree skirts

Fabric may be substituted for tree skirts. Whether or not you use fabric on the tree, you can buy several yards of fabric and loosely pool it under the tree. Nonstiff fabrics like satins and moirés work best. If you launder and press the fabric annually, it will look fresh every Christmas.

FABRIC AMOUNT

Use about 7 to 9 yards of fabric for a standard 7½-foot tree; when pooled on the floor, the fabric should extend beyond the longest branches.

1 Lay the fabric in a circle around the tree. Starting at the back, lift a piece of fabric and hang it over a bent green on a low branch. Choose a green halfway between the branch tip and trunk.

2 Continue this technique on every few branches until you go all the way around the tree, as seen on the finished tree above. Finish the look by loosely tucking the edges under, creating a soft, round appearance. For live trees, you should leave an opening in the back of the tree for watering.

TREE-SKIRT GALLERY

Note: see pages 187–89 for vendor information.

SATIN & SILK

1 Two-sided satin in hunter green and burgundy with gold-braid fringe

2 Hot-pink satin with pink marabou trim and ruffled, gold-specked taffeta

3 Gold-patterned brocade on white satin with thin gold-strand fringe

4 Ice-blue satin with ice-blue ruffled trim

5 Green satin with red-felt border and gold bric-a-brac

6 Burgundy silk dupione with beading and beaded border

VELVET & VELOUR

7 Hunter green and burgundy velvet brocade pie-wedge design with bric-a-brac and fringe

8 Lush red velvet with floral-taffeta pleated border

9 Aubergine velvet, reversible to purple satin, with gold-braid fringe

10 Red velvet with green sequin holly leaf and red berry appliqués with green border

11 Red velvet with braid accent in red, green, and gold

12 Leopard print velvet with gold-braid fringe

13 Red velour with gold-beaded snowflakes and gold-piping ties

14 Jewel-tone harlequin-pattern velvet with gold braiding and fringe

15 Solid black velvet with gold-braid fringe

TRADITIONAL MATERIALS

16 Red plush poly fur with hunter-green border

17 Green felt with white snowman appliqués and gold bric-a-brac border

18 Brown herringbone wool with beaded border and miniature silver jingle bells

19 Red felt with yarn pom-pom trim

TAKE-DOWN & STORAGE

"Striking the set"—also known as putting away the decorations—should be a breeze if you've prepared everything in advance. First, get out the trash bags, storage boxes, and/or totes. The way to "undecorate" is in reverse order of how you decorated. Strip your tree in this order: tree skirts, icicles, bows, beads and garlands, picks, ornaments, ribbon and fabric, statement pieces, treetops, and lastly, lights (for live trees and specialty light sets only). Ideally, you should store all Christmas items in a cool, dry place. Attic storage is the reason so many heirloom ornaments fade and mildew. Extremes in heat and humidity will damage every type of decoration.

▲ Tissues balls inserted into bow loops

bags in storage areas (attics, crawl spaces, garages, or lofts) on walls, from nails or hooks, or on racks. This can be a great space-saver. High temperatures damage fabric, so avoid attic storage in hot climates.

BEADS & GARLAND

Beads also need special care. Glass beads crush easily, and strands can tangle and become next year's nightmare. Carefully remove bead strands from the tree. Ideal storage is in the original manufacturer's box. Otherwise, wrap beads around a piece of cardboard or a plastic lighting-storage rack. Another inexpensive option is to wrap each bead strand

▼ Garland in its original cardboard box

around a paper-towel tube. This is not as effective for preventing tangling, but it's definitely better than piling all of your beads into one huge lump. Once they're wrapped, place the beads in a storage box.

We do not suggest plastic bags for bead storage, as the beads may be painted with a food-based paint, like many ornaments. If they are exposed to any humidity, the paint may bubble and peel off. Store light metallic garlands on top of other decorations. Artificial branch garlands should be loosely coiled and stored separately in cardboard boxes.

PICKS

Most picks don't require special attention. They shouldn't be placed at the bottom of a box of heavy decorations, but piling them into the corner of a storage box usually keeps them fresh-looking. If the picks are long and look like they might tangle, wrap them in paper towels. Glass picks should be packed carefully in tissue, like ornaments. Live fruit or flower picks should be thrown away, unless you want to dry them.

▲ A laundered, neatly folded tree skirt

TREE SKIRT

The skirt is the last item placed on (or actually under) your tree, and it should be the first item removed, so you won't step on it, soil it, or tear it. A skirt under a live tree can get damaged by water or sap: launder or dry clean it before packing it away for the year, so stains will not set permanently. Store your tree skirts in a cool, dry place, or try vacuum-sealed storage bags.

ICICLES

Tinsel icicles look best if they are fresh—you can try to pack them away carefully, but they crinkle easily, so it is best to buy new packs every year. Besides, they're inexpensive

and readily available. Plastic icicles don't need special care, but glass ones should be rolled in tissue paper before storage.

BOWS

Bows need special attention to look fresh for multiple-year use. Take single sheets of white tissue paper and gently crumple each sheet into a ball. Avoid using tinted tissue, which may bleed when damp. Remove bows from your tree one at a time. Insert a paper ball into each loop. Then place the bows gently into either storage boxes or large trash bags.

Bow boxes should be kept on top of all other decorations, since they are the lightest and most fragile items. You can hang

TAKE-DOWN & STORAGE

ORNAMENTS

Ornaments need the greatest care. They're your most valuable Christmas items and should be well protected. Remove metal ornament hooks before storing ornaments to avoid scratching. Newer plastic hooks are safer and can be left on, which will save you time next year.

▲ Protective ornament storage box

The safest storage is in boxes or tubs made specifically for ornaments. They usually come with cardboard inserts and keep ornaments individually protected. Even though some totes are made of plastic, they are still safe for long-term storage. The cardboard inserts absorb moisture in the air, and they aren't tightly sealed, which allows the ornaments to breathe, so they won't mildew.

If you live in an earthquake-prone area or will be moving the totes often, try using crushed white tissue paper under each ornament to provide an additional layer of protection.

If your space or budget is limited, wrap each ornament in plain paper, then carefully place them all in big cardboard boxes.

We use plain paper so that colors don't transfer. (Never use plastic or waxed paper. They both retain moisture and are harmful to all Christmas items.) This is also a safe way to care for less fragile ornaments, but even paper, clay, resin, Styrofoam, and plastic can crack under pressure.

Want to make your life easier? Use brightly colored permanent magic markers (red is a festive and appropriate color) to identify what you've packed. Write the word "Fragile" as well as a list of the contents on all of your Christmas-storage boxes, not just the ornament boxes; it will save you from having to keep opening the boxes throughout the year because you're wondering what's inside. And write this on all sides of the boxes, so that no matter how the box is stacked, you will be able to read the labels. Of course, those of you who are computer-savvy can always print up a stack of "Fragile: Christmas (fill in the blank)" signs, and tape them to every box.

RIBBON & FABRIC

Ribbon should be removed piece-by-piece and rerolled. Reroll the ribbon onto its original cardboard spool to keep it fresh from year to year. Start by attaching the end of the ribbon to the spool with cellophane tape. If it is "slippery" or doesn't stay rolled, secure each roll with a straight pin, a rubber band, or even baggie ties. However, don't roll it too tightly or it will crinkle. Fabric should also be removed at the same time. Launder it before storing.

STATEMENT PIECES & TREETOPS

To protect statement pieces and treetop decorations, try to store similar items together. Use several smaller boxes rather than one large one, to prevent pieces from being crushed or broken in the box. Layer the bottom of each box with lightly crushed balls of tissue paper—they will act as shock absorbers if the box gets jostled or dropped.

▼ Ribbon rerolled onto a spool

Gently wrap the head in tissue. If the hair is fibrous, take extra care so it won't get mussed in storage.

Wrap angels' hands in tissue to avoid chipping or peeling.

▲ A fragile angel

If you used wire to attach your pieces, remove it now so nothing will be scratched; fishing line is safe and can be left in place. Pictures and frames should be wrapped in layers of tissue or separated with sturdy corrugated cardboard, stood on end, and placed against one of the sides of the box. Wrap the hands and heads of dolls and angels in white tissue paper to prevent damage. Fragile angels should be the last items packed in the box.

Carefully wrap the electrical cords of any lit or animated piece. Collectibles like ceramic houses should definitely be packed back into their original boxes, not just for protection but also because keeping the original box adds to the value of the collectible.

LIGHTS

Lights need to be removed from live trees. To make it easier, plug them in and work in the reverse order of the way you added them to the tree.

Starting at the top, begin to pull lights off from the end that is not plugged in. Remove one string at a time, unplugging when you get to the plug end of each set of lights.

There are several simple and inexpensive storage techniques for lights that will prevent cord tangling. The easiest is self-wrapping in a ball, oblong, or cylinder. For the ball method, start at the end without the plug. Wrap the lights around your fingers a few times. Then continue to wrap the lights into a ball shape. When you reach the plug, tuck it under a wire and place the ball gently into a storage box.

The oblong method is similar; instead of making a ball, fold the lights to create a bunch with bulbs at each end (shown below, at right) and wrap them with their own cord. This is a great method for large bulbs like C-7s.

▼ Cylinder (below), ball (below left), and oblong (below right) light-storing methods

▲ Light spools in a storage bag

For the cylinder method, wrap the lights around an old paint roller or empty cardboard paper-towel tube. You can wrap lights around a flat piece of cardboard as well.

There are also a number of lightweight and inexpensive plastic frames on the market that make wrapping and storing lights quite easy, and they hold many light sets. You can wrap them as fully as you like: the idea is just to keep the cords from tangling.

For optimum storage, try storing your lights in plastic spools that come with their own storage bag. Lights are easily wrapped, and they are protected in breathable, durable bags—they unspool just as easily when it comes time to decorate your tree the following season.

Whether they are used on artificial or live trees, you should also remove specialty light sets. Bubble lights, flicker flames, and novelty lights can all become damaged if stored on an artificial tree. Remove the sets and wrap them in tissue if necessary.

TREES

Trees are "struck," or taken down, last. If you have a live tree, drain the tree stand with a suction pump or turkey baster. Then dry the inside of the bowl with a paper towel or rag to prevent dripping. If you placed a tree bag under the tree, pull it up, tie it at the top, and remove the tree. If not, be prepared to vacuum a trail of needles to the front door.

If you own an artificial tree, store it in its original box to keep it safe and free from dust and bugs. Don't pile anything heavy on top, especially if the tree is prelit. If the box will be stood on end, ensure that the treetop is in the top part of the box. Carefully position tree stands so they won't break under the weight of the tree.

▲ Bungeed artificial tree in original box

A prelit tree may no longer fit into its original box. Don't cram it in; instead, wrap one of the pieces separately and place in a smaller box or a tree bag.

To prepare your prelit tree for storage, first unplug the lights. Remove the treetop and lightly flatten it. Use bungee cords to help you fit your tree back into its box. Start at the top and tightly bungee rows one at a time. Be careful— bungee cords can hurt you if they snap loose. After one entire section is tightly bungeed, place it gently in the box.

▲ Set-up and rolled wall half-tree

Repeat for each section. Place extension cords and power strips in the box so they will be handy next year. You can also use bungees to seal the box.

Wall half-trees and collapsible spiral trees are easy to store: simply roll up the first and flatten the latter, and place them in a box.

The ornaments and ribbons are preattached to the tree

▲ Partially and fully collapsed spiral tree

SUPPLIERS

PARTS I & II

HERE IS IS A LIST OF ITEMS SEEN IN THE ROOM SETTINGS IN PART 1, AND IN THE DAMES' SETS IN PART 2. REFER TO PAGES 188–189 FOR DETAILED SUPPLIER CONTACT INFORMATION.

6–17 Majestic Statement
AMERICAN RIBBONZ LTD: Wired ribbon • ARCADIA HOME: Bead and ornament garlands • BARTHELMESS USA: Tree • CHRISTOPHER RADKO, INC: Silver bell with leaf pattern • DE ELENA COLLECTIONS: Clear Egyptian glass with 18-carat gold • GKI/ BETHLEHEM LIGHTS: Lights • MY CHRISTMAS WISH: Tree skirt • ORNA MENTZ: Small balls with pinned beads • POTTERY BARN: Wire heart with red beads • THE RHYN-RIVÉT COLLECTION, INC: Porcelain drops with poinsettia designs

18–19 Stunning Spiral
ARCADIA HOME: Beige beaded-fabric ornaments and beaded-silver star treetop

20–21 Victorian Influence
BETHANY LOWE DESIGNS, INC: Paper cone • DEPARTMENT 56: Lit village • ORNA MENTZ: Balls with fabric and pinned pearls • THE RHYN-RIVÉT COLLECTION, INC: Porcelain drops

22–23 Regal Banquet
CHERRY DESIGNS, INC: Heart with flower design • CHRISTOPHER RADKO, INC: Tree ornament with pastel decorations • FITZ AND FLOYD: Santa pitcher • MY CHRISTMAS WISH: Fabric-covered ball with tassel • ORNA MENTZ: Balls with fabric and pinned pearls • THE RHYN-RIVÉT COLLECTION, INC: Porcelains

24–25 Victorian Innocence
CHRISTINA'S WORLD: Father Christmas, blown-glass balls • MY CHRISTMAS WISH: Red fabric balls with white-fur trim • NEW EXPRESSIONS: Dolls and red hats • ORNA MENTZ: Balls with fabric and pinned pearls • TANNENBAUM TREASURES: Lit carved wood pieces • WALNUT RIDGE: Angel

26–27 Angelic Tableau
BROOKDALE COLLECTION: Angel • CHRISTINA'S WORLD: Mouth-blown-glass balls • MY CHRISTMAS WISH: Fabric covered balls with tassels and tree skirt • ORNA MENTZ: Balls with fabric and pinned pearls

30–31 Combined Traditions
J.P. BROWN: Bavarian and Swarovski crystal ornaments • THE RHYN-RIVÉT COLLECTION, INC: Porcelain drops

32–33 Elegant Ice
MY CHRISTMAS WISH: White ball with silver piping and tassel • THE RHYN-RIVÉT COLLECTION, INC: Porcelain drops

34–35 Christmas
BROOKDALE COLLECTION: Angels • MY CHRISTMAS WISH: Purple-velvet balls • ORNA MENTZ: Balls with fabric and pinned pearls • POLONAISE COLLECTION: Gold cross and trumpeting angel • SACRED SEASON: Handpainted mouth-blown-glass balls "Hosanna!" • VARSOVIA EASTERN EUROPE IMPORTS, INC: Camel, Magi ornament, and green swirly balls

36–37 Hanukkah
BARTHELMESS USA: Clear-and-blue shatterproof balls • DE ELENA COLLECTIONS: Blue-and-purple Egyptian glass with 18-carat gold • DEPARTMENT 56: Lit synagogue • EURO VUE: Blue Star of David • GROOVY HOLIDAYS: Felt bags • MITZVAHLAND: Crystal dreidel • SACRED SEASON: Handpainted blown-glass balls and eggs, and Star of Peace (charity) • TANNENBAUM TREASURES: Hanging eggs • WAXBERRY: Oil candles

38–39 Kwanzaa
ORNAMENTALS, INC: Handpainted blown-glass balls • TANNENBAUM TREASURES: Glass vegetables • ZAMBEZI BAZAAR: Kwanzaa items

42–43 Golden Opulence
BARTHELMESS USA: White tree and garlands • MY CHRISTMAS WISH: Fabric ornaments, sleigh, and tree skirts • ORNAMENTALS, INC: Hand-painted blown glass balls • ORNA MENTZ: Balls with fabric and pinned pearls • SACRED SEASON: Handpainted mouth-blown glass balls, white with gold "Hosanna!" • TANNENBAUM TREASURES: White angel with fur collar ornament •

VARSOVIA EASTERN EUROPE IMPORTS, INC: Long gold-and-silver ornaments and gold lion

44–45 Decadent Design
EURO VUE: Red heart • J.P. BROWN: Clear Bavarian and Swarovski crystal ornaments and pearl garlands • THE MICHAEL WEEMS COLLECTION, LLC: Etched glass candleholders • MY CHRISTMAS WISH: Velvet balls in black-and-leopard print and leopard sleigh • VARSOVIA EASTERN EUROPE IMPORTS, INC: Glass ornaments

46–47 Royal Velvet
AMERICAN RIBBONZ LTD: Wired ribbons • AUSTRIAN CHRISTMAS TREE: Clear glass balls with 18-carat gold • MY CHRISTMAS WISH: Velvet-covered balls with rope piping

48–49 Jewel-Tone Glamour
THE MICHAEL WEEMS COLLECTION, LLC: Etched martini glasses • VARSOVIA EASTERN EUROPE IMPORTS, INC: Glass ornaments

50–51 Crown Jewel
GOLDEN MOR INTERNATIONAL, INC: Suede table garland • THE MICHAEL WEEMS COLLECTION, LLC: Etched mini cocktail glasses • MY CHRISTMAS WISH: Pink tree skirt • ORNAMENTALS, INC: Painted glass balls • VARSOVIA EASTERN EUROPE IMPORTS, INC: Jewel-tone colored-glass ornaments

52–53 Dining Fantasy
AUSTRIAN CHRISTMAS TREE: Designer-inspired medallions and various-shaped ornaments • CHERRY DESIGNS, INC: Feather trees • DE ELENA COLLECTIONS: Tinted Egyptian glass with 18-carat gold • GOLDEN MOR INTERNATIONAL, INC: Jewel-tone candelabras • MY CHRISTMAS WISH: Gold silverware cozies and velvet-covered balls with rope piping • TANNENBAUM TREASURES: Eggs, glass-bead garlands

54–55 A Feast of Colors
AUSTRIAN CHRISTMAS TREE: Designer-inspired handpainted-glass medallions, hearts, and balls • CHERRY DESIGNS, INC: Feather

trees • CHRISTOPHER RADKO, INC: Gold finial holder • DE ELENA COLLECTIONS: Tinted Egyptian-glass with 18-carat gold • THE MICHAEL WEEMS COLLECTION, LLC: Etched glasses and red glass candles • MY CHRISTMAS WISH: Gold silverware cozies • TANNENBAUM TREASURES: Finial

58–59 Country Warmth
BETHANY LOWE DESIGNS, INC: Beige paper stars • BOARDWALK STUDIOS: Wood Santa and snowmen • CHERRY DESIGNS, INC: Glass cookies, candies, gingerbread men, and Santa • CHRISTIAN ULBRICHT: Nutcracker • GKI/BETHLEHEM LIGHTS: Lit holly bush • GROOVY HOLIDAYS: Decorative felt bags • INSPIRIO: Stuffed bears • MY CHRISTMAS WISH: Felt stockings • ORNAMENTALS, INC: Painted glass balls

60–61 Country Craftsmanship
BETHANY LOWE DESIGNS, INC: Standing snowman and beige-paper stars • CHERRY DESIGNS, INC: Glass candies, donuts, frosted cookies, gingerbread men, red reindeer, and white heart • GROOVY HOLIDAYS: Felt ornaments • MY CHRISTMAS WISH: Red felt stocking • ORNAMENTALS, INC: Painted glass balls • SACRED SEASON: Pears on red egg • TANNENBAUM TREASURES: Candle on a clip and pickle

62–63 European Country Buffet
BETHANY LOWE DESIGNS, INC: Wood Santa and seesaw • CHERRY DESIGNS, INC: Glass candy-and-cookie ornaments and gingerbread men • CHRISTIAN ULBRICHT: Nutcrackers • PARTYLITE: Gingerbread house with votive candle • PEGGY KARR GLASS: Dishes • SACRED SEASON: White egg with "The Holly and the Ivy" • TANNENBAUM TREASURES: Glass vegetables and wood pyramid

64–65 Holiday Hearth
AUSTRIAN CHRISTMAS TREE: Painted glass bell with 18-carat gold • BETHANY LOWE DESIGNS, INC: Moon and Santa decorations • CHERRY DESIGNS, INC: glass frosted leaves and stick candies •

(64–65 continued)
CHRISTIAN ULBRICHT: Nutcrackers • GKI/BETHLEHEM LIGHTS: Lit holly bush • SACRED SEASON: White egg with "The Holly and the Ivy" and blue ball with candles "Let Your Light Shine" • TANNENBAUM TREASURES: Glass pickle and vegetables

Pages 66–67 Winter Frost
ARCADIA HOME: Tree skirt • BETHANY LOWE DESIGNS, INC: Antiqued figurines and resin Father Christmas spinner game • GKI/BETHLEHEM LIGHTS: Snow-frosted tree • MY CHRISTMAS WISH: Fabric mittens and red-and-gold velvet-covered balls • POTTERY BARN: Pomegranate, large frosted cranberry balls, and garlands

68–69 Around the Fire
ARCADIA HOME: Tree skirt • BETHANY LOWE DESIGNS, INC: Antiqued figurines • BOARDWALK STUDIOS: Wooden Santa and deer • GKI/BETHLEHEM LIGHTS: Green wreath and garlands, lit berry topiary, and wreath • MICA SNOW: Antiqued snow • MY CHRISTMAS WISH: Stockings • PARTYLITE: Snowman skating rink and assorted glass candleholders • PEKING HANDICRAFT, INC: Pillows • TANNENBAUM TREASURES: Frosted fruit • VARSOVIA EASTERN EUROPE IMPORTS, INC: Cardinals, pinecones, and small balls with leaf pattern • WAXBERRY: Oil-jar candles

72–73 Northeast Chic
ABIGAIL'S COLLECTIONS: Red "Twelve Days of Christmas" balls • TANNENBAUM TREASURES: All other glass ornaments

74–75 Midwest Harvest
PEKING HANDICRAFT, INC: Nutcracker tassels • SACRED SEASON: Hand-painted red-and-white mouth-blown glass balls and eggs

76–77 Western Cornucopia
CHRISTINA'S WORLD: Hand-painted mouth-blown glass balls • POM WONDERFUL: Fresh pomegranates

78–79 Southern Elegance
CHRISTINA'S WORLD: Handpainted mouth-blown glass balls, purses, and shoes • JUST POTS: Decorative flowerpots

82–83 Retro Whimsy
DEPARTMENT 56: Lit houses • GKI/BETHLEHEM LIGHTS: Santa hat light sets • PARTYLITE: Motion snowglobe with votive

84–85 A Child's Party
CHERRY DESIGNS, INC: Glass crayons • CHRISTIAN ULBRICHT: Soldier nutcrackers • CHRISTOPHER RADKO, INC: "Shiny Brite" ornament line, elf-and-Santa-head platter, and Santa teapot • GROOVY HOLIDAYS: Felt gift bags • MY CHRISTMAS WISH: Felt silverware cozies and ornaments • PARTYLITE: Snow globe with votive • TANNENBAUM TREASURES: Santa nutcracker

Around the Tree
CHERRY DESIGNS, INC: Glass crayons, ducky pull-toy, giraffe, and tools • CHRISTOPHER RADKO, INC: Ceramic C-9 light-bulb sets, "Shiny Brite" ornament line • GROOVY HOLIDAYS: Felt gift bags • MY CHRISTMAS WISH: Felt silverware cozies/ornaments • A TOUCH OF GLASS: Stained-glass Santa ornament • VARSOVIA EASTERN EUROPE IMPORTS, INC: Glass fire engine

88–89 Looking In
CHRISTOPHER RADKO, INC: Novelty-light candelabras, bubble-light tree, and "Shiny Brite" ornament line • GKI/BETHLEHEM LIGHTS: Lit-berry wreath and Santa-hat lights • MEYDA TIFFANY: Lit stained-glass figures • PEGGY KARR GLASS: Glass plates and mini-plate ornaments

90–91 Small Quarters
CHERRY DESIGNS, INC: Glass sock monkey • CHRISTINA'S WORLD: Floral-decorated balls, white Santa head with fur • CHRISTOPHER RADKO, INC: Bells, caged angel, powder-blue retro refrigerator, and roly-poly snowman • DEPARTMENT 56: Train and depot • MATTARUSKY DESIGNS: Glittered whimsical molded-glass boy making snow angel and glass wreath • SLAVIC TREASURES: Large molded-glass candied balls

92–93 Tropical Delight
THE MICHAEL WEEMS COLLECTION, LLC: Hurricane candleholder • ORNAMENTALS, INC: Painted glass balls • ORNAMENTS TO REMEMBER: Hawaiian-themed molded glass—coconut, flip-flops, Hawaiian shirts, luggage tag, octopus, "paradise egg," sea horse, seashells, snow cone, and tropical fish • TANNENBAUM TREASURES: Bird-of-paradise, clip-on flower, pineapples, and sliced fruit • VARSOVIA EASTERN EUROPE IMPORTS, INC: Flamingos

94–95 Island Flavor
AMERICAN RIBBONZ LTD: "Electric ribbon" • ORNAMENTS TO REMEMBER: Hawaiian-themed molded glass—Hawaiian shirt, "paradise egg," and tropical fish • TANNENBAUM TREASURES: Hummingbird

Pages 96–97 Alternative Style
CHERRY DESIGNS, INC: Feather trees and purple glass candy • CHRISTINA'S WORLD: Frosty eggs with decorative pink glitter • ORNAMENTALS, INC: Zebra-print handpainted white glass balls • VARSOVIA EASTERN EUROPE IMPORTS, INC: Glass silver bells

98–99 Fashion Colors
BARTHELMESS USA: Black and pink trees • CHRISTINA'S WORLD: Handpainted silver glass balls • MY CHRISTMAS WISH: Tree skirt • EDIE BASKIN-BRONSON: photographs • POTTERY BARN: Wire heart with clear crystal beads and treetop star

100 Travelers' Tree
CHRISTIAN ULBRICHT: Nutcracker • CHRISTOPHER RADKO, INC: Finials, "Shiny-Brite" line • DEPARTMENT 56: Lit houses • GKI/BETHLEHEM LIGHTS: Lights • PEGGY KARR GLASS: Glass mini ornaments, platters • POLONAISE COLLECTION: Glass Egyptian figures

101 Topsy-Turvy
GROOVY HOLIDAYS: Felt bags • HARBOUR LIGHTS: Hot-air balloons • MATTARUSKY DESIGNS: Glittered molded-glass figurines • ORNAMENTALS, INC: Handpainted glass balls

102–3 Storytelling
Haunted Holiday—ARCADIA HOME: Felt garland • CHERRY DESIGNS, INC: Black cat, candy corn, ghost, and witch's hat • MATTARUSKY DESIGNS: Glittered Jack o' lantern-man • ORNAMENTALS, INC: Handpainted glass balls

Wildlife Treasures—AMERICAN RIBBONZ LTD: Wired faux-fur ribbon • BARTHELMESS USA: Pink tree • BETHANY LOWE DESIGNS, INC: Glittery silver stars • SLAVIC TREASURES: Collectible glass wild-animal heads

Red Hat Society—AUSTRIAN CHRISTMAS TREE: Designer-inspired purple glass ball and shapes • NEW EXPRESSIONS: Doll and red fabric hats • SACRED SEASON: Purple egg with gold harp "The Book of Psalms" • TANNENBAUM TREASURES: Purple perfume bottles

Bridal Memories—J.P. BROWN: Bavarian and Swarovski crystal ornaments • THE RHYN-RIVÉT COLLECTION, INC: Porcelain drops • SACRED SEASON: White glass ball with gold design "Hosanna!"

108–9 Elizabeth Taylor
POLONAISE COLLECTION: Egyptian-glass ornaments

110–11 Joan Crawford
ARCADIA HOME: Beige beaded ornaments, tree skirt (used as cape) • CHERRY DESIGNS, INC: eight-point stars • HISTORY FOR HIRE: Mannequin head • J.P. BROWN: Pearl garlands • VARSOVIA EASTERN EUROPE IMPORTS, INC: Glass coach and swan

112 Marilyn Monroe
BARTHELMESS USA: White Christmas tree • CHRISTINA'S WORLD: Pink eggs • JOY TO THE WORLD: Pink Christmas-tree ornament

113 Lana Turner
HISTORY FOR HIRE: Hatboxes and mannequin heads • HOLLYWOOD HISTORY MUSEUM: Lana's compact and dress • ORNAMENTALS, INC: White balls with zebra stripes • VARSOVIA EASTERN EUROPE IMPORTS, INC: Decorative glass balls

114–15 Lucille Ball
HISTORY FOR HIRE: Combs and hairbrushes • MY CHRISTMAS WISH: Fabric balls • VARSOVIA EASTERN EUROPE IMPORTS, INC: Glass ornaments

116–17 Judy Garland
CHRISTOPHER RADKO, INC: Large red glass ornaments with gold swirls • HISTORY FOR HIRE: Microphone, steamer trunk • POLONAISE COLLECTION: Ruby slippers and *Wizard of Oz* figures • SACRED SEASON: Red handpainted, mouth-blown glass ball "Pentecost" • VARSOVIA EASTERN EUROPE IMPORTS, INC: Rainbow glass balls

118–19 Bette Davis and Katharine Hepburn
ORNA MENTZ: Ornaments in Bette's headdress • SACRED SEASON: Red glass egg • VARSOVIA EASTERN EUROPE IMPORTS, INC: Glass ornaments on "Kate"

SUPPLIERS' ADDRESSES

ABIGAIL'S COLLECTIONS
c/o Tannenbaum Treasures
20 Research Parkway
Old Saybrook, CT 06475
T: 866-395-1801
F: 860-395-1802
email: jpfeffer01@snet.net
www.tannenbaumtreasures.com
Ornaments: mouth-blown
glass; "12 Days of Christmas"
series balls

ALEX THEATRE
216 North Brand Boulevard
Glendale, CA 91203
T: 818-243-2611
Landmark theater

AMERICAN RIBBONZ LTD.
2543 North Hancock
Philadelphia, PA 19133
T: 215-425-3273
F: 215-425-3481
email: yackma2@aol.com
Ribbon: custom-designed,
wired ribbon

ANGELA'S
Christopher Radko's
Starlight Store
2329 Michael Drive
Newbury Park, CA 91320
T: 800-617-2356
email: info@radko.net
www.radko.net
Ornaments: blown glass,
Halloween; Table decorations

ARCADIA HOME
New York, NY
T: 212-787-3282
F: 212-787-3281
info@arcadiahomeinc.com
www.arcadiahomeinc.com
Ornaments: fabric; Ribbon
(beaded); Tree skirts and
runners (beaded)

AUSTRIAN CHRISTMAS TREE
P.O. Box 5753
Manchester, NH 03104
T: 603-668-6377
F: 603-627-6783
austrianchristmas@comcast.net
www.austrianchristmastree.com
Ornaments: blown glass

BARTHELMESS USA
T: 800-227-2262
www.barthelmessusa.com
Light covers; Shatterproof
ornaments; Trees: full-sized,
tabletop, "fashion firs,"
prelit, and unlit; Wreaths,
green garlands, and
"fashion garlands"

BETHANY LOWE DESIGNS, INC.
16655 County Highway 16
Osco, IL 61274
T: 800-944-6213
F: 309-944-3205
www.bethanylowe.com
Ornaments: paper, resin, tin,
and wood; Pillows; Table
decorations: vintage

BOARDWALK STUDIOS
P. O. Box 358
Bristol, IN 46507
T: 574-848-4183
F: 574-848-7579
Wooden decorations; Full-size
snowman and Santa plaques

BROOKDALE COLLECTION
brookdale@enter.net
www.brookdalecollection.com
Angels

CHERRY DESIGNS, INC.
12319 F. M. 1960 East
Huffman, TX 77336
T: 800-918-9140
F: 281-324-2399
cherry@cherrydesignsinc.com
www.cherrydesignsinc.com
Ornaments: molded glass,
Halloween-themed; Trees:
multicolored feather trees

CHRISTINA'S WORLD
27 Woodcreek Ct.
Deer Park, NY 11729
T: 631-242-9664
F: 631-586-1918
www.christinasworld.com
Ornaments: blown glass

CHRISTIAN ULBRICHT
www.ulbricht.com
Nutcrackers

CHRISTOPHER RADKO, INC.
see ANGELA'S

DÉCOR DIMENSIONS
105 Skegby Rd.
Brampton, ON
L6V 2T8 Canada
T: 905-455-5904
Ornament hooks: adjustable,
spiral hooks

DE ELENA COLLECTIONS
P. O. Box 4239
Irvine, CA 92616
T: 949-786-3231
Ornaments: Egyptian glass

DEPARTMENT 56
T: 800-548-8696
www.d56.com
Lit buildings: seasonal
accessories and collectibles;
Snow effects: artificial snow

DONALD CLAY DESIGNS
P. O. Box 1391
Running Springs, CA 92382
T: 818-642-1523
Floral design

DR. CHRISTMAS RENTS, INC.
1209 West Isabel Street
Burbank, CA 91506
T: 818-840-0445
F: 818-848-5923
www.drchristmas.com
dr_Christmas@hotmail.com
Props

EURO VUE
2370 Rice Boulevard
Houston, TX 77005
T: 713-520-0224
www.europevillage.com
Ornaments: molded glass

GKI / BETHLEHEM LIGHTS
www.gkilights.com
Lights; Tree: rustic, snowy-style

**GOLDEN MOR
INTERNATIONAL, INC.**
T: 562-531-4800
F: 562-531-4848
www.goldenmor.com
Table decorations: jeweled
candelabras

GROOVY HOLIDAYS
T: 212-625-1301
F: 212-625-0146
www.groovychristmas.com
Fabric bags

HAND & HAMMER SILVERSMITHS
2610 Morse Lane
Woodbridge, VA 22192
T: 800-745-8379
www.hand-hammer.com
Ornaments: metals

HARBOUR LIGHTS
1000 North Johnson Avenue
El Cajon, CA 92020
T: 800-365-1219
www.harbourlights.com
Ornaments: hot-air balloons

HISTORY FOR HIRE
7149 Fair Avenue
North Hollywood, CA 91605
T: 818-765-7767
www.historyforhire.com
historyforhire@aol.com
Props

**HOLLYWOOD HISTORY MUSEUM
HISTORIC MAX FACTOR BUILDING**
1660 North Highland Avenue
Hollywood, CA 90028
T: 323-464-7776
www.hollywoodhistory
museum.org
Museum

INSPIRIO
5300 Patterson Avenue, S.E.
Grand Rapids, MI 49530
T: 866-231-8239
www.inspiriogifts.com
Teddy bears

JOY TO THE WORLD
T: 877-676-2636
jttwcoll@aol.com
www.joytotheworldonline.com
Ornaments: molded glass

J.P. BROWN
c/o Younger & Associates
1000 North Johnson Avenue
El Cajon, CA 92020
T: 800-365-1219
www.harbourlights.com
Ornament hooks: decorative,
with crystals or pearls;
Ornaments: Bavarian &
Swarovski crystal

JUST POTS
755 South Wall Street
2nd Floor
Los Angeles, CA 90014
T: 213-623-4344
theorchidman@hotmail.com
Floral containers: decorative florist pots

KURT S. ADLER, INC.
www.kurtadler.com
Ornaments: resin, tin, wood

LARRY FRAGA DESIGNS
140 Fulton Street
Fresno, CA 93721
T: 559-441-8000
larryfragadesign@aol.com
www.larryfragadesigns.com
Ornaments: blown and molded

MARK KLAUS
P.O. Box 470758
Broadview Heights, OH 44147
Clayman63@aol.com
Ornaments: resin

MATTARUSKY DESIGNS
Chicago, IL
T: 630-469-4125
F: 630-469-5017
mattarusky@msn.com
www.mattarusky.com
Ornaments: molded glass, Halloween

MEYDA TIFFANY
T: 800-222-4009
info@meyda.com
www.meyda.com
Lit sculptures

MICA SNOW
22921 Belquest Dr.
Lake Forest, CA 92630
T: 949-581-6422
F: 949-581-6442
cordie@micasnow.com
www.micasnow.com
Snow effects: vintage snow

THE MICHAEL WEEMS COLLECTION, LLC
1103 North Washington Street
1st Floor
Baltimore, MD 21213
T: 410-327-9500
F: 410-327-9600
www.michaelweems.com
Glassware: goblets, flutes, martinis, and hurricanes

MITZVAHLAND
16733 Ventura Boulevard
Encino, CA 91436
T: 818-705-7700
www.mitzvahland.com
Hanukkah: Judaica

MR. GREENTREES
310-276-9827
Live trees, wreaths, and garlands

MY CHRISTMAS WISH
Bartlett, TN
T: 901-373-2229
www.mychristmaswish.net
Ornaments: fabric; Tree skirts and runners

NE'QWA ART
545 N. Cowan, Bldg. J
Lewisville, TX 75057
T: 877-821-8635
F: 972-219-9850
custom@neqwa.com
www.neqwa.com
Ornaments: blown glass

NEW EXPRESSIONS
2004@yahoo.com
Dolls; Ornaments: red hats

ORNAMENTALS, INC.
Tuscaloosa, AL
T: 205-349-3915
ornament@dbtech.net
www.ornamentalsinc.com
Ornaments: blown glass and Halloween-themed

ORNAMENTS TO REMEMBER
T: 800-330-3382
info@ornaments2remember.com
www.ornamentstoremember.com
Ornaments: molded glass

ORNA MENTZ
308 Victoria Ave.
Wilmington, DE 19804
sales@ornamentz.com
www.christmasballs.com
Ornaments: fabric

PARTYLITE
c/o Valerie Hayden
T: 805-520-0522
Candles

PEGGY KARR GLASS
100 Washington Street
Randolph, NJ 07869
T: 800-754-8585, x23
F: 973-659-1220
tseitz@peggykarrglass.com
www.peggykarrglass.com
Glassware: plates, platters, and dishware; Ornaments: fused glass

PEKING HANDICRAFT, INC.
1388 San Mateo Avenue
So. San Francisco, CA 94080
T: 800-872-6888
www.pkhc.com
Pillows: needlepoint; Rugs

POLONAISE COLLECTION
polonaise@kurtadler.com
www.kurtadler.com
Ornaments: molded glass

POM WONDERFUL
11444 W. Olympic Boulevard
Los Angeles, CA 90064
T: 310-966-5800
F: 310-966-5801
www.pomwonderful.com
Pomegranates

POTTERY BARN
T: 888-779-5176
www.potterybarn.com
Ornaments: metals, plastic

THE RHYN-RIVÉT COLLECTION, INC.
Brooklyn, WI 53521
T: 866-835-7886
www.rhyn-rivet.com
Ornaments: porcelain

RICHARD ROCHA
T: 323-440-2433
kameakuke@sbcglobal.net
Gourmet pastry chef

SACRED SEASON
P.O. Box 1744
Tuckerton, NJ 08087
T: 866-872-6635
www.4GloriousGifts.com
Ornaments: blown glass

SEASONAL CONNECTION
2810 Upland Avenue
Lubbock, TX 79407
T: 806-792-2429
www.ezupfasttrax.com
Ornament hooks: green-plastic "Ultimate"

SLAVIC TREASURES
T: 877-752-8428
SlavicT@aol.com
www.slavictreasures.com
Ornaments: molded glass

TANNENBAUM TREASURES
20 Research Parkway
Old Saybrook, CT 06475
T: 866-395-1801
F: 860-395-1802
jpfeffer01@snet.net
www.tannenbaumtreasures.com
Garlands: glass; Ornaments: molded glass; Treetops: glass finials; Wood: carved arches, pyramids, and nutcrackers

A TOUCH OF GLASS
4342 Via Alegre
Yorba Linda, CA 92886
T: 714-701-0632
Ken@Touch-of-Glass.com
www.touch-of-glass.com
Stained-glass artwork: Santa "ornament"

VARSOVIA EASTERN EUROPE IMPORTS, INC.
8037 Churchill Avenue, #1
Niles, IL 60714
T: 847-966-9903
F: 847-966-9469
varsovia1@aol.com
www.varsovia-ornaments.com
Ornaments: blown and molded glass

WALNUT RIDGE
www.walnutridge.com
Table decorations

WAXBERRY
909 East Fox Farm Road, #7
Cheyenne, WY 82007
T: 888-824-4006
F: 307-772-9850
www.waxberry.com
Candles; Decorative oil jars

YESTERYEARS TREASURES
Kathi@YesteryearsTreasures2004.com
Ornaments: red hats

ZAMBEZI BAZAAR
4334 Degnan Boulevard
Los Angeles, CA 90008
T: 323-299-6383
F: 323-299-2574
www.jzambezik@aol.com
Kwanzaa: gifts

INDEX

Note: Photographs are indexed by page of caption.

PHOTOGRAPHY CREDITS

t=top; b=bottom; l=left; r=right; c=center
All photographs © David Mager/DK Picture Library except:

6tl: © Jeff Katz; 8c (photo inside frame): © RoseMary Staron;
8br: © Brad Fowler, Song of Myself Studio; 9tr: © Jim Stewart,
luckyshotsphoto.com
137 (chart): Norway spruce & scotch pine © Dave King/DK Picture
Library; Noble fir © Stephen Hayward/DK Picture Library;
Eastern white pine © Sue Oldfield/DK Picture Library; Austrian pine
© Matthew Ward/DK Picture Library
139tr (monofilament): © Steve Gorton and Andy Crawford/DK
Picture Library; 139tr (hooks): © Dave King/DK Picture Library
161 (Fabric Gallery): 1 & 8 © Laura Knox/DK Picture Library;
4 © Mark Harwood/DK Picture Library; 5 © Sue Baker/
DK Picture Library

ACKNOWLEDGMENTS

AUTHORS' ACKNOWLEDGMENTS
Thanks to the following people who contributed in many varied ways
throughout our pursuit of Christmas glory.

For no particular reason, other than the fact that both of *our*
names start with letters nearer to the end of the alphabet than the
beginning, our list appears in reverse alphabetical order:

Stars / Locations
Robert and Rosemary Stack, Debbie Reynolds, Steve Radosh, Steve
Nycklemoe, John Murphy, Barry McComb, BeBe McCloud, Linda
Marder, Tim Malachosky, Elizabeth Lamont, Deidre Hall, Merv
Griffin, Faye Grant, Whoopi Goldberg, Peri Gilpin, Andy and Marivi
Garcia, Jo Jo Dellit, Donelle Dadigan, Steven Collins, Casa de Flores,
Tom Bergeron, Peter Barthelmess, Ann and Steve Arvin, Vincent
Arcuri, Beth Anderson, Kirstie Alley, Kristian Alfonso

Family
Ted and RoseMary Staron, Robert and Betty Pranga, Maurice and
Louise Pippenger, Nancy Flowers, Sally and Koti

Suppliers
Kris Wilson, Tina Van Oss, Kathie Underwood, Gertrude Theriault,
Shirley Strzemieczny, Sarah Stanley, Michael Solomon, Tim's
Snowmaker, Wendy Shick, Tim Seitz, Michael Salomon, Kurt &
Barbara Salomon, Mike Robinson, Katherine Reinert, Christopher
Radko, Chris Quintos, Chris Puleo, Ken Pollack, Tom Poddebski, Jim
Pfeffer, T. J. Persia, Ellen McGuire, Barbara McClay, Ann and Matt
Litavsky, Mark Klaus, Lisa Kelechava, Joi Jibotian, Ashleigh Hanninen,
Caryl Hamilton, Ray Hamby, Roger Gruen, Larry Fraga, Pam Elyea,
Paulie Drissi, Mandy Del Rosario, Susan Cotter, Susan Cherry, Diane
Carnevale-Jones, Mary Margaret Cannon, Kent Brown, Christine
Bertucci, Barbara Bartoloni

Press / Contacts
Ken and Janet Zitterer, Susan Turner, Mark Stuplin, Michelle Stranahan,
Loren Ruch, Bob Rosenblatt, Avery Roberts, Brent Ries, Jonathan
Renes, Mark Rafalowski, Sue Procko, Christopher Pica, Quinn
Monahan, Craig Modderno, Janice Lucas, Christopher Lowell, John
Kip, Brent Hopkins, Cynthia Hayes, Harutune Hamassian, Lisa
Gleason, Mary Ford, Jeffrey Epstein, Gabriele Edgell, Barry Diller,
Bob and Helen Collier, Brandon Castillo, Kelly Carter, Gary Bryan,
Grace Bradberry, Mark Bozek, Judy Blye-Wilson, Carol Bidwell,
Jim Beckmann

Hair & Makeup (miracle workers!)
Sherri Simmons, Valerie Riccardi, Joe Jadeski, Michael Haumesser

Friends
Ann Wilson, Lynn Underwood, Donna Sloane, Tony Rosato, Otilia
Orellana, Chris Monte, Donna Miller, Matt Mgee, Fern McMillan,
Charley McCarley, Charles May, Maria Loverde, Mark Lohmann,
Vicki Larkin, Gayla Hope, Jim Haynes, Tom Godfrey, Rob Freud,
Sandy Dvore, Brian Conn, Elizabeth Campbell, Suzanne Boothe

Elves
Eric Woodard, Scott West, Lisa Teitelman, Jeff Taylor, Mike Pingel,
Tim Maculean, Molly Lewis, Donna Lackey, Dayna Jackson, Owen
Eden, Nelson Davila, Michael Dashiell, John Dallas, Bill Clark,
Frank Bonventre

DK Publishing
Cathy Melnicki, Sharon Lucas, Chuck Lang

Photographer David Mager

. . . and Santa, without whom none of this would have been possible!

PUBLISHERS' ACKNOWLEDGMENTS
DK Publishing would like to thank the following people for
their invaluable help: Leeza Gibbons, for the wonderful foreword;
David Mager, for his stunning photographs and for his patience and
dedication both on set and off; and indefatigable photographer's
assistants Monica Morant, Beth Coller, and Charchi Stinson. We are
indebted to the gracious homeowners and business owners in Los
Angeles who opened their doors to our crew. Special thanks go to
Donald Clay, for his beautiful floral designs, and Richard Rocha, for
his delicious culinary creations.

We are also grateful to Dr. Christmas "Elves" Garry Kubel, Jay
Krich, Lynn Klein, Gail Jorden, Brent Braun, and Brent Bateman
for their assistance on set; Jacqueline Olson, Insurance Claims
Administrator, and Wendy Cornell, Risk and Insurance Manager, at
Pearson for so kindly providing needed forms at a moment's notice;
Stuart Calderwood, John Searcy, and Shira Bistricer for their
editorial help; Tai Blanche, Melissa Chung, Susan St. Louis, Stephanie
Sumulong, and Miesha Tate for assisting with the design; Josephine
and Catherine Yam, Colourscan, for the spectacular reproductions;
Nanette Cardon, IRIS, for the index; and Sterling Youngman and
David Zellorford for their prop loan.